COOK SMART **entertaining**

Healthy and delicious food for every occasion

SIMON & SCHUSTER

A CBS COMPANY

First published in Great Britain by Simon & Schuster UK Ltd, 2010
A CBS Company

Copyright © 2010, Weight Watchers International, Inc.
Simon & Schuster Illustrated Books, Simon & Schuster UK Ltd, First Floor, 222 Gray's Inn Road, London WC1X 8HB

Weight Watchers and *POINTS* are trademarks of Weight Watchers International, Inc., and are used under its control by Weight Watchers (UK) Ltd.

Weight Watchers Publications: Jane Griffiths, Nina McKerlie.

Recipes written by: Sue Ashworth, Sue Beveridge, Tamsin Burnett-Hall, Cas Clarke, Siân Davies, Roz Denny, Becky Johnson, Kim Morphew, Joy Skipper, Penny Stephens and Wendy Veale.

Photography by: Iain Bagwell, Steve Baxter, Steve Lee and Juliet Piddington
Design and typesetting by Tiger Media Ltd.
Printed and bound in China

A CIP catalogue for this book is available from the British Library

ISBN 978-1-84737-936-8

1 3 5 7 9 10 8 6 4 2

Pictured on the front cover: Stuffed Acorn Squash p140, Chicken Satay Skewers p111, Creamy Garlic Chicken p135, Chocolate Roulade p80
Pictured on the back cover: Lemon and Blueberry Charlottes p75, Cheesy Chicken Goujons p 114, Prawn and Avocado Salad p 35, Cream Hearts with Passion Fruit p148
Pictured on the introduction: Herb Loaf p44, Chocolate Mousse p116, Roasted Vegetable Bruschetta p69, Tomato, Thyme and Goat's Cheese Tartlets p100

 POINTS ® value logo: You'll find this easy to read *POINTS* value logo on every recipe throughout this book. The logo represents the number of *POINTS* values per serving each recipe contains. Weight Watchers offers you a healthy and sustainable way to lose weight.
For more information about Weight Watchers call 08457 123 000 or visit www.weightwatchers.co.uk

V   This symbol denotes a vegetarian recipe and assumes that, where relevant, free range eggs, vegetarian cheese, vegetarian virtually fat free fromage frais, vegetarian low fat crème fraîche and vegetarian low fat yogurts are used. Virtually fat free fromage frais, low fat crème fraîche and low fat yogurts may contain traces of gelatine so they are not always vegetarian. Please check the labels.

✱   This symbol denotes a dish that can be frozen.

Recipe notes
Egg size: Medium, unless otherwise stated.
All fruits and vegetables: Medium sized, unless otherwise stated.
Raw eggs: Only the freshest eggs should be used. Pregnant women, the elderly and children should avoid recipes with eggs that are not fully cooked or raw.
Stock: Stock cubes used in recipes, unless otherwise stated. These should be prepared according to packet instructions.
Recipe timings: These are approximate and meant to be guidelines. Please note that the preparation time includes all the steps up to and following the main cooking time(s).
Low fat spread: Where a recipe states to use a low fat spread, a light spread with a fat content of no less than 38% should be used.

Contents

Introduction

Welcome to a new way of looking at party food with the help of Weight Watchers. Many people think party food is fatty and full of calories, but *Cook Smart Entertaining* is here to prove otherwise. It is filled with healthy and delicious recipes, all of which are specially selected from the best of Weight Watchers cookbooks and are sure to be a hit with all your friends and family.

From simple ideas for two to finger food for up to 20, from a Bonfire Night party to a romantic supper, there is something here for all occasions. We have provided some menu ideas at the start of each chapter but there are many more combinations – try mixing and matching the recipes throughout this book to create the perfect menu. *Cook Smart Entertaining* is the best way to make sure your special occasion goes perfectly.

About Weight Watchers

For more than 40 years Weight Watchers has been helping people around the world to lose weight using a long term sustainable approach. Weight Watchers successful weight loss system is based on four tried and trusted principles:

- Eating healthily
- Being more active
- Adjusting behaviour to help weight loss
- Getting support in weekly meetings

Our unique **POINTS** system empowers you to manage your food plan and make wise recipe choices for a healthier, happier you.

Basic Ingredients

Milk

Always use skimmed milk, rather than whole or semi-skimmed, unless otherwise stated in the recipe.

Eggs

Use medium sized eggs, unless otherwise stated in the recipe. Always bring eggs to room temperature before using. A cold egg won't whisk well and the shell will crack if placed in hot water.

Fats and Oils

The majority of recipes use low fat cooking spray rather than oil. Low fat cooking spray can be either olive oil or sunflower oil based. Try both and see which you prefer.

Cheese and Yogurt

The cheese used in these recipes is low fat Cheddar, low fat soft cheese or virtually fat free fromage frais. Many recipes use yogurt. Always choose either 0% fat Greek yogurt or low fat natural. All of these products are easy to find in a supermarket.

Fruit and Vegetables

Make sure your family eats plenty of fruit and vegetables, preferably at least five portions a day. Filling up on fruit and vegetables can also stop you from feeling hungry, so you are less likely to snack on fatty and sugary foods.

Planning Ahead

When you're going around the supermarket it is tempting to pick up foods you like and put them in your trolley without thinking about how you will use them. So, a good plan is to decide what dishes you want to cook before you go shopping, check your store cupboard ingredients and make a list of what you need. You'll save time by not drifting aimlessly around the supermarket picking up what you fancy. You might even have time for a cup of tea or coffee.

Store Cupboard Suggestions

apricots, canned
artichokes, canned
artificial sweetener
baking powder
broad beans, frozen
bulgar wheat
butter beans, canned
capers in brine
chick peas, canned
chilli (flakes, powder, paste)
chocolate
    (spread, 70% cocoa, white)
cinnamon sticks
cloves
cocoa powder, unsweetened
coconut milk, reduced fat
cornflour
couscous
cranberries. frozen
cream of tartar
curry paste (red, green)
custard, low fat ready made
digestive biscuits, reduced fat
dried fruit (apple pieces, apricots,
    sultanas, raisins, currants)
flageolet beans, canned
flour (plain, self raising)
fish sauce, Thai
garlic (cloves, purée)
ginger (fresh root, pickled, purée)
golden syrup
haricot beans, canned

herbs, dried (mixed, oregano,
    thyme, mint, bay leaves)
honey, runny
horseradish sauce
kaffir lime leaves
kidney beans, canned
lemongrass
lentils, Puy
low fat cooking spray
mango chutney
mayonnaise, low fat
mushrooms, dried
mustard (English mustard
    powder, Dijon, wholegrain)
noodles, rice
nuts (walnuts, hazelnuts,
    pistachio, cashew, pecan,
    whole and flaked almonds)
oats, porridge
oil (olive, sesame, vegetable)
olives (in brine)
pasta
peanut butter, crunchy
peas, frozen
peppercorns
peppers, bottled
pesto
pineapple, canned
pizza base mix
prawns, frozen
rice (brown, long grain, sushi,
    mixed wild and basmati,
    risotto)

saffron
salt (sea salt or low sodium)
seafood, frozen
sesame seeds
Shredded Wheat
soy sauce, dark
spices, ground (mixed, coriander,
    cumin, Chinese 5 spice,
    paprika, cinnamon, ginger,
    nutmeg, cayenne pepper,
    garam masala)
spices, seeds (caraway, coriander,
    cumin)
sponge fingers
stock cubes (vegetable, chicken,
    fish, beef)
sugar (brown, soft light brown,
    icing, golden caster, demerara,
    light and dark muscovado)
sweet chilli sauce
sweetcorn, frozen
tomato purée
tomato salsa
tomatoes, canned
tortillas, flour
tuna, canned in spring water
vanilla (essence, extract)
vinegar (balsamic, white wine,
    rice)
wasabi paste
Worcestershire sauce

Lunches and Picnics

Menu Ideas

Veggie lunch Potato and Celeriac Soup (p12), Carrot and Butter Bean Terrine (p32) and Apple and Raspberry Filo Tart (p38).

Family picnic Potted Peppered Mackerel (p19), Tangy Potato Salad (p34), Herb Loaf (p44) and Orange Raspberry Bites (p39).

Lunch with a friend Falafel with Minted Yogurt (p18) and Pistachio Biscotti (p40).

Sunday lunch Deluxe Prawn Cocktail (p10), Italian Roast Chicken (p14) and Tiramisu (p36).

Mix and match recipes for great lunch and picnic ideas

Deluxe Prawn Cocktail

White crabmeat, rocket and asparagus give this traditional favourite an upmarket new twist.

Serves 4

¼ Iceberg lettuce, shredded
25 g (1 oz) rocket leaves
100 g (3½ oz) asparagus tips, halved
12 cherry tomatoes, quartered
175 g (6 oz) small prawns, defrosted
170 g can white crabmeat in brine, drained
cayenne pepper

For the cocktail sauce
2 tablespoons low fat mayonnaise
2 tablespoons low fat natural yogurt
2 tablespoons tomato ketchup
½ tablespoon lime juice
2 tablespoons skimmed milk
salt and freshly ground black pepper

2 **POINTS** values per serving
8 **POINTS** values per recipe

C 126 **calories** per serving

Takes **7 minutes** to prepare,
3 minutes to cook

✳ not recommended

1 Toss the lettuce and rocket together and divide between four glass dishes or plates.

2 Bring a pan of water to the boil and cook the asparagus for 3 minutes, then drain and refresh under a cold tap. Drain again. Scatter the asparagus and cherry tomatoes over the salad. Divide the prawns and crabmeat between the dishes.

3 To make the cocktail sauce, mix the mayonnaise, yogurt, ketchup and lime juice together with some seasoning in a small bowl, then gradually whisk in the milk until smooth.

4 Drizzle the sauce over each dish just before serving and add a dusting of the cayenne pepper.

Potato and Celeriac Soup

A great way of ensuring you get your quota of greens.

Serves 4

low fat cooking spray
350 g (12 oz) potatoes, peeled and cut
    into chunks
350 g (12 oz) celeriac, peeled and cut
    into chunks
1 large onion, chopped
1 garlic clove, crushed
1 green chilli, de-seeded and chopped
    finely (optional)
200 g (7 oz) winter greens (i.e. Savoy cabbage
    or green cabbage), shredded finely
1.2 litres (2 pints) hot vegetable stock
salt and freshly ground black pepper

1 **POINTS** value per serving
4 **POINTS** values per recipe

C **115 calories** per serving

Takes **10 minutes** to prepare,
35 minutes to cook

V

✻ recommended

1. Heat a large, lidded, non stick saucepan, spray with the cooking spray and add the potatoes, celeriac, onion, garlic and chilli, if using. Cover and cook over a gentle heat for 10 minutes, shaking the pan occasionally, until the vegetables have softened without colouring.

2. Meanwhile, bring a pan of water to the boil and add the shredded greens. Cook for just 3–4 minutes until wilted. Drain and refresh the greens under cold running water then drain thoroughly. Set aside.

3. Add the stock to the potatoes and celeriac, season, bring up to simmering point and simmer gently, covered, for 20 minutes, or until the vegetables are very tender.

4. Liquidise the soup until smooth using a blender or hand held blender. Return to the saucepan together with the wilted greens and reheat gently. Check the seasoning before serving, piping hot.

Tips Choose your favourite winter greens for this recipe. Shredded Brussels sprouts and spinach are also delicious and full of flavour at this time of year. The **POINTS** values remain the same.

Unless freezing, use the soup within a day or two of making as the celeriac does tend to discolour slightly.

Variations Omit the chilli if you prefer a milder level of heat – but be generous when adding freshly ground black pepper.

For a non vegetarian version, chicken stock gives a good depth of flavour, for the same **POINTS** values.

Savoury Pasta Slices

These slices are delicious hot or cold and perfect to pop in a picnic hamper.

Serves 6

low fat cooking spray
a bunch of spring onions, chopped finely
90 g (3¼ oz) small pasta shapes
90 g (3¼ oz) lean cooked ham, chopped
90 g (3¼ oz) mature half fat Cheddar
  cheese, grated
3 eggs, beaten
1 tablespoon chopped fresh mixed herbs,
  or 1 teaspoon dried herbs
salt and freshly ground black pepper

2½ *POINTS* values per serving
16 *POINTS* values per recipe

146 calories per serving

Takes **20 minutes** to prepare,
30 minutes to cook + cooling

✱ recommended

1 Preheat the oven to Gas Mark 5/190ºC/fan oven 170ºC. Spray a 20 cm (8 inch) cake tin with the cooking spray.

2 Bring a small amount of water to the boil, add the spring onions and cook for 3–4 minutes.

3 At the same time, bring a second pan of water to the boil and cook the pasta for 8–10 minutes, until just tender. Drain the spring onions and pasta, then leave to cool slightly.

4 Mix together the spring onions, pasta, ham, cheese, eggs and herbs. Season well then transfer to the prepared tin. Level the surface.

5 Bake for about 30 minutes, until firm and golden. Allow to cool completely before removing from the tin, then cut into six wedges. To keep for later, wrap the slices tightly in foil or greaseproof paper.

Italian Roast Chicken

This recipe shows you how to give a tasty twist to the traditional roast that the whole family will love. Serve with a crisp, green, zero **POINTS** value salad and a medium (225 g/8 oz) jacket potato per person, for an extra 2½ **POINTS** values per serving.

Serves 4

8 x 85 g (3¼ oz) skinless boneless chicken thighs, trimmed of fat
2 teaspoons low fat spread
2 teaspoons mild chilli powder
½ teaspoon dried oregano or basil
½ teaspoon salt
freshly ground black pepper
a lemon, quartered, to serve

7½ **POINTS** values per serving
27½ **POINTS** values per recipe

C **222 calories** per serving

Takes **5 minutes** to prepare, **25 minutes** to cook

✱ not recommended

1 Arrange the chicken thighs in a shallow baking dish. Preheat the oven to Gas Mark 4/180°C/fan oven 160°C.

2 Beat together the low fat spread, chilli powder, herbs and salt. Dab this mixture on top of the chicken thighs.

3 Season the chicken with pepper and then cover the baking dish loosely with foil. Bake for 20–25 minutes, until the chicken is tender and cooked through.

4 Divide the chicken between four serving plates. Pour over any remaining cooking juices and serve each portion with a lemon quarter.

Pastrami and Sticky Onion Wraps

Fabulous for a picnic. Wrap the filled tortillas in greaseproof paper or cling film to stop them from drying out.

Serves 2

1 onion
½ teaspoon olive oil
2 soft flour tortillas
60 g (2 oz) low fat soft cheese
25 g (1 oz) wild rocket
4 slices pastrami
salt and freshly ground black pepper

4 POINTS values per serving
7½ POINTS values per recipe

252 calories per serving

Takes **2 minutes** to prepare,
8 minutes to cook

✱ not recommended

1 Preheat the grill to medium.

2 Cut the onion into 10 or 12 wedges, slicing through the root so that the sections stay together. Place in a small roasting tin and drizzle with the oil and 3 tablespoons water. Season and toss to coat.

3 Cook under the preheated grill for 6–8 minutes, turning once. The liquid will evaporate, softening the onions as they cook.

4 Meanwhile, gently warm the tortillas to soften them, either by dry frying for 15 seconds on each side, or by warming in the microwave for 15 seconds.

5 Spread each tortilla with half the soft cheese, then scatter on the rocket. Add the onions and two slices of pastrami each. Fold in one edge to form a base for the wrap, then roll up tightly.

Falafel with Minted Yogurt

A good recipe for picnics or lunch with a friend, these spiced chick pea patties can be served either warm or at room temperature on a bed of crisp lettuce, diced cucumber and tomato, with the minted yogurt drizzled on top.

Serves 2

100 g (3½ oz) low fat natural yogurt
¼ teaspoon dried mint, plus a pinch extra
410 g can chick peas, rinsed and drained
1 teaspoon ground coriander
1 teaspoon ground cumin
1 egg white
2 spring onions, chopped
low fat cooking spray
salt and freshly ground black pepper

1 Mix the yogurt together with the ¼ teaspoon dried mint and seasoning and set aside for the flavour to develop.

2 Tip the chick peas into a food processor, adding the extra pinch of dried mint, spices, egg white, spring onions and seasoning. Whizz until quite finely processed, but with a few chunky pieces of chick pea remaining.

3 Bring the mixture together in a ball, then shape into eight small patties, using damp hands if the mixture is sticky.

4 Heat a non stick frying pan and spray with the cooking spray. Add the patties and cook for 3 minutes on each side over a medium heat until crisp and well browned. Serve the falafels with the minted yogurt.

2½ *POINTS* values per serving
5 POINTS values per recipe

180 calories per serving

Takes 9 minutes to prepare,
6 minutes to cook

V

* recommended for falafel only

Potted Peppered Mackerel

This tasty pâté is a lunchtime favourite. Serve with a zero **POINTS** value salad and a medium (225 g/8 oz) jacket potato per person, for an extra 2½ **POINTS** values per serving, or with 2 medium (35 g/1½ oz) slices of toast per person, for an extra 2½ **POINTS** values per serving.

Serves 6

220 g can butter beans, rinsed and drained

200 g (7 oz) peppered mackerel fillets, skinned

1 large red onion, chopped very finely

1 garlic clove, crushed (optional)

finely grated zest and juice of a lemon

1 tablespoon chopped fresh parsley

salt and freshly ground black pepper

To garnish

parsley sprigs

lemon slices

1 Tip the butter beans into a large mixing bowl and use a potato masher or fork to mash to a purée. Add the mackerel fillets and flake roughly with a fork, then stir into the beans.

2 Add most of the red onion, reserving a little for garnish. Add the garlic (if using), lemon zest, lemon juice and parsley. Season, then mix together thoroughly.

3 Divide the mixture between six small ramekin dishes. Cover and chill until ready to serve, then garnish with parsley, lemon slices and the reserved red onion.

2½ **POINTS** values per serving
14½ **POINTS** values per recipe

C 145 calories per serving

Takes **10 minutes**

* recommended

Tip For a smooth pâté, whizz together all the ingredients in a food processor, or use a hand held blender, for 15 seconds.

Variations Canned chick peas or cannellini beans can be used instead of butter beans. These are best when puréed in a blender. The **POINTS** values will remain the same.

For a decorative starter that doesn't add further **POINTS** values, use the pâté to fill hollowed-out tomatoes.

Chicken and Apple Coleslaw

A tasty, all-in-one meal, which is a variation on a traditional favourite. You can serve the coleslaw immediately, or it will keep for at least 12 hours in a fridge.

Serves 4

100 g (3½ oz) low fat soft cheese
1 teaspoon Dijon mustard
6 tablespoons low fat natural yogurt
2 teaspoons lemon juice
200 g (7 oz) white cabbage, shredded finely
100 g (3½ oz) carrots, peeled and grated
¼ red onion, diced finely
250 g (9 oz) cooked skinless boneless chicken breasts, shredded
1 apple, cored and sliced thinly
2 Little Gem lettuces, leaves separated
8 cherry tomatoes, halved
salt and freshly ground black pepper
4 parsley sprigs (optional), to garnish

3 *POINTS* values per serving
11½ *POINTS* values per recipe

C   **203 calories** per serving

Takes **15 minutes** to prepare

✳   not recommended

1 Beat the soft cheese, mustard, yogurt and lemon juice together in a small bowl or jug. (A mini whisk is very useful to get a smooth consistency.)

2 Place the prepared cabbage, carrots, onion, chicken and apple in a large mixing bowl and add the soft cheese mixture. Mix thoroughly and season to taste.

3 When ready to serve, place the lettuce leaves around the edges of four shallow bowls and put a quarter of the coleslaw in the centre of each bowl. Serve topped with the tomatoes and if you're using parsley, sprinkle it over before serving.

Tip Use the soft cheese mixture as a dressing for other salads, instead of mayonnaise.

Variations This coleslaw has a creamy taste. If you prefer a sharper flavour, increase the mustard and lemon juice a little. The ***POINTS*** values will remain the same.

V For a vegetarian variation, drain a 400 g tin of butter beans and substitute these for the cooked chicken, for 2 ***POINTS*** values per serving.

Caramelized Onion and Polenta Slice

Polenta makes a perfect light lunch side dish.

Serves 8

200 g (7 oz) dried polenta
low fat cooking spray
1 kg (2 lb 4 oz) onions, sliced finely
a small bunch of fresh marjoram, oregano or parsley, chopped
4 large beefsteak tomatoes, sliced
salt and freshly ground black pepper

1 Cook the polenta as instructed on the packet and then pour into a deep 20 cm (8 inch) springform cake tin and allow to cool.

2 Heat a large, lidded, non stick frying pan or wok and then spray with the cooking spray.

3 Add the onions and stir fry for a few minutes before turning the heat to low and covering the onions with a sheet of baking parchment and a lid. Cook the onions for 30 minutes, until soft and caramelized, stirring occasionally to ensure that they don't burn.

4 Preheat the oven to Gas Mark 4/180°C/fan oven 160°C.

5 Sprinkle the herbs, reserving some to garnish, over the polenta, then tip in the onions and spread over. Top with the tomatoes and season. Bake for 20 minutes.

6 Remove from the tin, scatter with the reserved herbs and cut into eight slices to serve.

1½ **POINTS** values per serving
10 POINTS values per recipe

C **143 calories** per serving

Takes **20 minutes** to prepare, **50 minutes** to cook

V

* not recommended

Thai Beef Salad

A tasty salad with a hint of spice that makes a great light lunch or a starter for a supper party.

2½ POINTS VALUE

Serves 4

For the dressing

1 shallot, diced very finely
1 garlic clove, crushed
2 tablespoons chopped fresh
coriander
½ red chilli, de-seeded and diced
very finely
1½ tablespoons lime juice
1 tablespoon fish sauce
½ tablespoon brown sugar

For the beef salad

300 g (10½ oz) beef fillet
1 teaspoon sesame oil
2 tablespoons chopped fresh
coriander
1½ tablespoons fresh mint,
chopped
75 g (2¾ oz) bag mixed salad
leaves
½ cucumber, sliced thinly
8 cherry tomatoes, halved

1   Make the dressing by putting all the ingredients into a jar and
    shaking well. Chill in the fridge until required.

2   Preheat the grill to a medium high heat. Use a pastry brush to brush
    the steak with the sesame oil. Grill for 3 minutes on each side. (Or, if
    you prefer, you can pan fry the steak with the oil.) Leave to one side
    to let the meat rest while you prepare the salad.

3   Share out all the remaining salad ingredients between four plates.
    Slice the beef as thinly as possible and lay it on top of the salad.
    Pour the dressing over the meat and salad then serve.

2½ **POINTS** values per serving
9½ **POINTS** values per recipe

C 161 calories per serving

Takes **15 minutes** to prepare,
10 minutes to cook

* not recommended

Tip Traditionally the steak used in this dish is served rare. You can of
course adjust the cooking time of the meat to suit your preference;
5–7 minutes each side will give a medium to well done steak.

Spanakopita

This Greek dish is equally good hot or cold and perfect for taking on a picnic.

Serves 2

low fat cooking spray
1 onion, sliced thinly
2 garlic cloves, crushed
300 g (10½ oz) spinach
a kettle full of boiling water
50 g (1¾ oz) reduced fat Feta cheese, cubed
1 egg, beaten
½ teaspoon caraway seeds
8 x 15 g sheets filo pastry
  (30 x 18 cm/12 x 7 inches)
salt and freshly ground black pepper

4 POINTS values per serving
8½ POINTS values per recipe

C **321 calories** per serving

Takes **35 minutes** to prepare,
25–30 minutes to cook

V

✱ not recommended

1 Lightly coat a non stick frying pan with the cooking spray and heat until hot. Add the onion, reduce the heat and cook for 10 minutes until beginning to brown. Stir in the garlic and cook for a further 2 minutes. Remove from the heat.

2 Preheat the oven to Gas Mark 6/200°C/fan oven 180°C.

3 Place the spinach in a colander and pour over the boiling water. Drain, cool and squeeze out any excess liquid with the back of a wooden spoon before chopping roughly.

4 Mix the spinach and onions together with the cheese, egg and caraway seeds. Season.

5 Spray a sheet of filo pastry with the cooking spray and lay on a baking tray. Spray another and lay it beside the first, but just overlapping, to make a square. Repeat with two more sheets, laying them the opposite way, but on top. Place the spinach mixture in the middle and spread to within 5 cm (2 inches) of the edge. Fold up the edges and then top with two more sheets of sprayed filo pastry. Seal the edges. Repeat with two more sheets and then spray the whole thing before baking for 25–30 minutes until golden.

Blue Cheese Salad with Crispy Rashers and Croûtons

Rocket has the most wonderful flavour, and tastes delicious with crumbled blue cheese and crispy cooked turkey rashers.

Serves 4

4 turkey rashers
2 tablespoons lemon juice
1 teaspoon wholegrain mustard
1 bag of rocket leaves, rinsed
175 g (6 oz) young spinach leaves, rinsed
75 g (2¾ oz) blue Stilton, crumbled
4 tablespoons low fat natural yogurt
2 teaspoons chopped fresh herbs (e.g. chives,
    parsley or oregano)
4 tablespoons garlic and herb croûtons
salt and freshly ground black pepper

3½ *POINTS* values per serving
14 *POINTS* values per recipe

C 185 calories per serving

Takes **10 minutes** to prepare,
5 minutes to cook

* not recommended

1 Preheat the grill to medium. Arrange the turkey rashers on the grill pan.

2 Mix 1 tablespoon of lemon juice with the mustard and brush over the rashers. Grill for 2 minutes on each side, until browned. Allow to cool slightly.

3 Meanwhile, divide the rocket and spinach leaves between four serving bowls and sprinkle with the remaining lemon juice.

4 Snip the turkey rashers into fine shreds and sprinkle over the leaves. Add the blue cheese.

5 Mix the yogurt with the herbs and pour over the salads. Sprinkle the croûtons on top, season and serve.

Salade Niçoise

Salade Niçoise has a delicious combination of ingredients in it and makes a substantial meal in itself.

Serves 4

2 eggs
250 g (9 oz) new potatoes, scrubbed and halved
  if large
150 g (5½ oz) green beans, trimmed
150 g (5½ oz) mixed salad leaves
8 olives in brine
1 red onion, sliced
200 g (7 oz) canned tuna in spring water, drained
2 tomatoes, quartered

For the dressing
1 tablespoon olive oil
juice of ½ a lemon
½ teaspoon Dijon mustard
salt and freshly ground black pepper

2½ *POINTS* values per serving
10½ *POINTS* values per recipe

210 **calories** per serving

Takes **20 minutes** to prepare,
20 minutes to cook

* not recommended

1 Bring a small saucepan of water to the boil, add the eggs and simmer for 8 minutes. Remove the eggs from the pan and place under cold running water for 3–4 minutes to prevent the yolks from turning grey.

2 Bring a second pan of water to the boil and cook the potatoes for 10 minutes, then add the beans. Cook for a further 6–8 minutes until the potatoes and beans are tender. Drain and leave to cool slightly.

3 Shell the eggs and cut them into quarters.

4 In a salad bowl, gently toss together the salad leaves, olives, onion, potatoes and beans.

5 Fork the tuna over the top of the salad and top with the egg quarters and tomatoes.

6 For the dressing, whisk together the olive oil, lemon juice and Dijon mustard. Season to taste.

7 Pour the dressing over the salad and serve immediately.

Greek Chicken in Pitta

Want to feel as if you're back on a sunny beach? You may not get the weather, but this recipe should bring you all the right flavours.

Serves 4

2 tablespoons lime juice
1 teaspoon coriander seeds, crushed
1 teaspoon ground cumin
2 tablespoons chopped mint
250 g (9 oz) skinless boneless mini chicken fillets
100 g (3½ oz) reduced fat houmous
100 g (3½ oz) 0% fat Greek yogurt
¼ Iceberg lettuce, shredded
½ red onion, cut into rings
1 red pepper, de-seeded and sliced
4 tomatoes, quartered
½ cucumber, diced
20 black olives in brine, pitted
8 mini pitta breads

4½ **POINTS** values per serving
18½ **POINTS** values per recipe

271 calories per serving

Takes **20 minutes**

✳ recommended for chicken and unfilled pittas only

1 In a bowl, mix the lime juice with the coriander seeds, cumin and a tablespoon of the mint. Roll the chicken fillets in this to coat and put on one side until ready to cook.

2 Mix together the houmous and the Greek yogurt.

3 Preheat a grill to a medium to hot temperature. Meanwhile, arrange the lettuce, onion, pepper, tomatoes, cucumber and olives on a plate or in a bowl. Sprinkle with the remaining chopped mint.

4 Grill the chicken for 5 minutes on each side, or until the meat is cooked through. A few minutes before the end of the cooking time, put the mini pittas under the grill and toast on each side for a minute or two. Alternatively, you can toast the pittas in a toaster.

5 Cut the chicken fillets in half lengthways and open the pittas by splitting them halfway round the edge. Fill the pittas with the chicken fillets and half of the houmous mix. Serve accompanied by the salad and the remaining houmous mix.

Broad Bean, Ham and Pasta Salad

A summery salad that is great for picnics.

Serves 4

50 g (1¾ oz) dried pasta
225 g (8 oz) fresh or frozen broad beans
225 g (8 oz) thick sliced lean ham, cut into 1 cm (½-inch) cubes
a packet of fresh mint, chopped

For the dressing
zest and juice of a lemon
1 teaspoon olive oil
1 teaspoon honey
1 teaspoon wholegrain mustard
salt and freshly ground black pepper

3 *POINTS* values per serving
11½ *POINTS* values per recipe

160 calories per serving

Takes **15 minutes** to prepare,
12 minutes to cook

✱ not recommended

1 Bring a pan of water to the boil, add the pasta and cook according to packet instructions. Drain and set aside.

2 Half fill another large pan with water and bring to the boil. Add the broad beans and cook for 2 minutes, then drain. Run under cold water and drain again. Now the skins should just pop off when you squeeze the bean between thumb and forefinger, revealing a bright green bean. Put the beans in a serving bowl with the ham, mint and pasta.

3 Put all the dressing ingredients together in a jam jar, screw on the lid and shake vigorously. Pour over the pasta mix and toss.

Tip The broad beans can be served whole but they have a better texture and flavour if they are skinned.

Rice and Vegetable Lunch Pot

This tasty mixture of brown rice and vegetables is equally delicious eaten hot or cold. Pack it in a plastic container for a filling and tasty lunchtime or picnic snack.

Serves 4

225 g (8 oz) dried brown rice
225 g (8 oz) carrots, peeled and diced
1 onion, chopped
1 green pepper, de-seeded and diced
1 red pepper, de-seeded and diced
150 g (5½ oz) mushrooms, sliced
2 tablespoons dark soy sauce
700 ml (1¼ pints) vegetable stock
2 tablespoons tomato purée
100 g (3½ oz) frozen peas

3 POINTS values per serving
12½ POINTS values per recipe

290 calories per serving

Takes **25 minutes** to prepare,
45 minutes to cook

V

✳ recommended

1 Place the rice in a large, lidded saucepan with the carrots, onion, peppers and mushrooms. Mix together the soy sauce, stock and tomato purée, and then add this mixture to the rice and vegetables.

2 Bring everything to the boil. Reduce the heat, cover and simmer gently for 35 minutes, stirring from time to time.

3 Stir in the frozen peas. Cover and cook for a further 5–10 minutes, until all the liquid has been absorbed and the rice is tender.

4 Serve warm, or chill in the fridge and serve as a rice salad.

Variation Try adding a tablespoon of curry powder to the rice while it is cooking, to add a hint of spice. The **POINTS** values will remain the same.

Carrot and Butter Bean Terrine

This colourful terrine is delicious eaten hot or cold. Serve it with a simple, zero **POINTS** value sliced tomato salad drizzled with balsamic vinegar.

Serves 4

700 g (1 lb 9 oz) carrots, peeled and diced
1 onion, chopped
1 garlic clove, crushed
600 ml (1 pint) vegetable stock
1 teaspoon ground coriander
2 large eggs
25 g (1 oz) fresh white or wholemeal
  breadcrumbs
420 g can butter beans, rinsed and drained
150 g (5½ oz) low fat soft cheese with garlic
  and herbs
salt and freshly ground black pepper

3½ **POINTS** values per serving
13 **POINTS** values per recipe

C **250 calories** per serving

Takes **45 minutes** to prepare,
1 hour to cook

V

✱ recommended

1 Place the carrots, onion, garlic and stock in a large, lidded saucepan and bring to the boil. Add the ground coriander and seasoning. Cover and simmer for 15 minutes until the carrots are tender. Drain well and mash thoroughly or blend in a food processor. Beat in the eggs and stir in the breadcrumbs.

2 Line a 900 g (2 lb) loaf tin with non stick baking parchment. Spoon half the mixture into the tin.

3 Mash the butter beans with the soft cheese or blend them together in a food processor. Spread this over the carrot mixture in the tin. Top with the remaining carrot mixture.

4 Cover the terrine with a sheet of non stick baking parchment, and then cover the whole tin with foil.

5 Place the tin in a large, lidded saucepan or wok and pour in enough water to come half way up the sides of the tin. Bring the water to the boil, cover and reduce the heat. Simmer gently for 1 hour. Check the water level from time to time and top up with boiling water if necessary. Alternatively, preheat the oven to Gas Mark 5/190°C/fan oven 170°C, place the tin in a roasting tray with water halfway up the sides and bake for 1 hour.

6 Carefully lift the tin out of the water, remove the foil and baking parchment and let it cool.

7 Run a round bladed knife around the edge of the terrine to loosen the edges. Place a serving platter on top of the tin, and then turn the tin upside down so the terrine drops out on to the platter. Cut it into eight slices and serve two slices per person.

Tangy Potato Salad

A lighter, tastier version of the heavy, traditional mayonnaise or salad cream potato salad.

Serves 6

1 kg (2 lb 4 oz) new potatoes, chopped into bite size chunks
10 radishes, sliced
a small bunch of chives, chopped finely
150 g (5½ oz) low fat natural yogurt
1 tablespoon low fat mayonnaise
salt and freshly ground black pepper

1 Bring a large saucepan of water to the boil, add the potatoes and boil for 15–20 minutes, until tender, then drain thoroughly.

2 Place the potatoes in a large bowl with the remaining ingredients and mix together. Serve warm or cold.

2 POINTS values per serving
13½ POINTS values per recipe

140 calories per serving

Takes **5 minutes** to prepare, **20 minutes** to cook

V

✳ not recommended

Prawn and Avocado Salad

A delicious indulgent lunch – perfect for when you are saving some of your **POINTS** allowance for something later in the day.

Serves 4

1 cucumber, ends removed
2 Little Gem lettuces, shredded
a bunch of watercress
1 avocado
256 g (9 oz) king prawns, cooked and peeled
a box of salad cress
1 lemon, quartered

1 Cut the cucumber in half lengthways. Then cut it lengthways again to get four long pieces. Cut these into 5 mm (¼ inch) thick slices.

2 Mix the cucumber with the shredded lettuce and watercress and divide between four plates.

3 Cut the avocado in half, peel off the skin and remove the stone. Halve again lengthways and slice into chunks similar in shape and size to the cucumber. Scatter this on to the lettuce mixture.

4 Top with the prawns and a sprinkling of salad cress. Garnish with a lemon quarter to squeeze over as a dressing.

2 **POINTS** values per serving
8½ **POINTS** values per recipe

C 124 calories per serving

Takes **10 minutes**

＊ not recommended

Tip This salad also makes an ideal starter – it would serve six as a starter with a **POINTS** value of 1½ per serving.

Variation The lemon juice really brings out the flavour of the prawns and contrasts well with the creamy avocado, but if you prefer a different dressing, try a fat free vinaigrette for no extra **POINTS** values.

Tiramisu

This is a delicious low **POINTS** values version of the famous Italian dessert.

Serves 4

8 sponge fingers
1 tablespoon granulated artificial sweetener
3 tablespoons Marsala wine
1 tablespoon instant coffee, dissolved in 3 tablespoons hot water
350 g (12 oz) 0% fat Greek yogurt
1 egg white
25 g (1 oz) plain chocolate with 70% cocoa solids, grated, to serve

2 **POINTS** values per serving
8½ **POINTS** values per recipe

C 260 calories per serving

Takes **25 minutes** + at least **1 hour** chilling

V

✳ recommended

1 Divide the sponge fingers between four individual shallow glass dishes.

2 Stir the sweetener and Marsala wine into the dissolved coffee. Drizzle the coffee mixture equally over the sponge fingers.

3 Place the yogurt in a mixing bowl. Whisk the egg white until it forms soft peaks and fold it into the yogurt. Spoon this over the soaked sponge fingers.

4 Cover and chill the dishes for at least 1 hour or overnight. Sprinkle the top of each tiramisu with grated chocolate just before serving.

Variations For a lemon version of this recipe, replace the coffee granules and water with 3 tablespoons of freshly squeezed lemon juice. Sprinkle the tops with finely grated lemon or orange zest. The **POINTS** values will be 1½ per serving.

If you can't find Marsala wine, use brandy instead. The **POINTS** values will be 2½ per serving.

Apple and Raspberry Filo Tart

This delicious light tart makes a wonderful finish to a lunch with friends.

Serves 4

800 g (1 lb 11 oz) cooking apples, peeled, cored and sliced
100 ml (3½ fl oz) orange juice
15 x 15 g sheets (28½ x 43½ cm/11¼ x 17¼ inches) filo pastry
low fat cooking spray
100 g (3½ oz) fresh raspberries
1 teaspoon icing sugar, to dust
2 tablespoons half fat crème fraîche, to serve

1 Preheat the oven to Gas Mark 6/200°C/fan oven 180°C.

2 In a saucepan, simmer the apples in the orange juice for 8–10 minutes, until just tender.

3 Spray six sheets of filo pastry with the cooking spray and overlap to cover the base of a 23 cm (9 inch) loose bottomed tart tin. Cook in the oven for 5 minutes.

4 Remove the tart tin from the oven and fill with the apples and raspberries, but don't add too much juice.

5 Spray the remaining sheets of filo then scrunch them up and arrange on the top of the fruit.

6 Bake for another 15–20 minutes until golden brown.

7 Dust with icing sugar and serve each portion with ½ tablespoon of crème fraîche.

4½ **POINTS** values per serving
17½ **POINTS** values per recipe

C **275 calories** per serving

Takes **15 minutes** to prepare, **25 minutes** to cook

V

* not recommended

Orange Raspberry Bites

These fruity little cakes will appeal to everyone – delicious with a cup of tea or coffee.

Makes 6

zest of an orange
2 teaspoons cornflour
250 g (9 oz) ricotta cheese
3 eggs, beaten
75 g (2¾ oz) golden caster sugar
50 g (1¾ oz) fresh raspberries

1 Preheat the oven to Gas Mark 3/160°C/fan oven 140°C and line a six hole non stick muffin tin with muffin cases.

2 In a bowl, whisk together the orange zest, cornflour, ricotta, eggs and sugar until smooth.

3 Divide the mixture between the muffin cases and top each with two or three raspberries in the centre. Bake in the oven for 30–35 minutes until golden and set.

4 Leave to cool in the tin, then remove and serve.

3½ POINTS values per serving
22 POINTS values per recipe

C **160 calories** per serving

Takes **10 minutes** to prepare,
35 minutes to cook + cooling

V

* not recommended

Pistachio Biscotti

Biscotti means 'twice baked' and that's exactly what happens to these crunchy biscuits, which are great for dipping into coffee. They can be stored in an airtight container for up to a week.

Makes 10

110 g (4 oz) plain flour
½ teaspoon baking powder
50 g (1¾ oz) low fat spread
zest of ½ an orange
75 g (2¾ oz) soft light brown sugar
50 g (1¾ oz) chopped pistachios
1 teaspoon instant coffee, dissolved in
  2 teaspoons hot water
1 egg white

1½ *POINTS* values per serving
16 *POINTS* values per recipe

C 115 calories per serving

Takes **15 minutes** to prepare,
45 minutes to bake + **15 minutes** cooling

V

✱ not recommended

1 Preheat the oven to Gas Mark 4/180°C/fan oven 160°C. Line a baking tray with non stick baking parchment.

2 Sift the flour and baking powder into a large bowl. Add the low fat spread and rub in until it resembles breadcrumbs. Stir in the orange zest, sugar and pistachios.

3 Add the dissolved coffee and egg white and knead to a soft dough, adding a little water if it is too dry.

4 Shape the dough into a log 5 cm (2 inch) wide and 5 cm (2 inch) high. Place on the baking tray and bake for 35 minutes until golden and firm.

5 Remove from the oven and cool for 15 minutes on the baking tray and then cut into 10 slices. Lay them side down on the baking tray and bake again for 10 minutes until golden.

Variation Try using chopped almonds instead of the pistachios, for 2 **POINTS** values per serving.

Scottish Shortbread

This shortbread has all the flavour of the traditional butter versions but is low in fat.

Makes 24

225 g (8 oz) polyunsaturated margarine
125 g (4½ oz) caster sugar
50 g (1¾ oz) ground rice
225 g (8 oz) plain white flour
a pinch of salt
1 teaspoon caster sugar, for sprinkling

1 Preheat the oven to Gas Mark 4/180°C/fan oven 160°C and line a baking sheet with non stick baking parchment.

2 Place the margarine, sugar and ground rice on a board and, with your fingertips, draw them together until thoroughly mixed.

3 Combine the flour and salt. Add the flour by sprinkling it over in four batches and incorporating it each time with your fingertips but avoid over working the mixture.

4 Roll or pat out the mixture to 5 mm (¼ inch) thickness and then cut into rounds with a 5 cm (2 inch) cutter. Place the rounds on the prepared baking sheet and bake for 15 minutes, until golden brown. Sprinkle the teaspoon of caster sugar over all the shortbread and then cool on a wire rack.

2½ **POINTS** values per serving
58 **POINTS** values per recipe

C   **130 calories** per serving

Takes **15 minutes** to prepare,
15 minutes to cook

V

✱   not recommended

Tip It helps to keep the mixture cool or else it may become too sticky. The mixture can be refrigerated for 10 minutes or so before rolling out if it is too difficult.

Apple and Cinnamon Flapjacks

These little bites are great for picnics, the lunch box or to just sit and nibble at leisure.

Makes 12 squares

100 g (3½ oz) low fat spread
75 g (2¾ oz) dark muscovado sugar
2 tablespoons golden syrup
175 g (6 oz) porridge oats

1 teaspoon ground cinnamon
75 g (2¾ oz) dried apple pieces, chopped into bite size pieces
25 g (1 oz) raisins or currants

1 Preheat the oven to Gas Mark 5/190°C/fan oven 170°C.

2 In a pan, heat together the low fat spread, sugar and syrup until melted and well blended.

3 Mix in the oats, cinnamon, apple pieces and raisins or currants.

4 Spread the mixture in an 18 cm (7 inch) shallow square, non stick tin. Bake for 15 minutes.

5 Leave to cool in the tin before marking into 12 squares. Once completely cold, remove from the tin and store in an airtight container.

2½ *POINTS* values per serving
27½ *POINTS* values per recipe

145 calories per serving

Takes **10 minutes** to prepare, **15 minutes** to cook + cooling

V

* recommended

Tips Measure out syrup using a hot metal spoon if you require 'tablespoons', or by placing the tin of syrup on to the scales and subtracting the required amount from the starting weight as you spoon out the syrup.

Dried apple can be found in health food shops and in most supermarkets in the baking section.

Variation Replace the apple with 50 g (1¾ oz) mixed dried fruit. Allow 2 *POINTS* values per square.

Herb Loaf

This is based on the French 'Cake aux Herbes' and is enjoyed as a lunch dish or handed around in small pieces with drinks. Serve with a zero **POINTS** value green salad.

Serves 6 (2 slices each)

low fat cooking spray
150 g (5½ oz) low fat spread, melted and cooled slightly
2 eggs, separated
150 g (5½ oz) self raising flour
2 garlic cloves, crushed
25 g (1 oz) green and black olives in brine, chopped
1½ tablespoons capers in brine, rinsed
5 tablespoons freshly chopped mixed herbs, e.g. parsley, chives, sage, tarragon, thyme, dill, basil
2 egg whites

3½ **POINTS** values per serving
21½ **POINTS** values per recipe

C 211 calories per serving

Takes **15 minutes** to prepare, **30 minutes** to cook + **10 minutes** cooling

V

* recommended

1 Preheat the oven to Gas Mark 4/180°C/fan oven 160°C. Lightly coat a 900 g (2 lb) loaf tin with the cooking spray.

2 Pour the melted low fat spread into a large bowl and beat in the 2 egg yolks. Add the flour and beat in with the garlic, olives, capers and herbs.

3 In a clean, grease free bowl, whisk all the egg whites until they hold stiff peaks and then gradually fold into the other mixture.

4 Spoon into the prepared tin and bake for 30 minutes until golden and set – a skewer inserted in the centre should come out clean. Cool for 10 minutes in the tin before turning out.

5 Serve warm or cold.

Tip Store in an airtight container in the fridge for up to 3 days.

Special Evenings

Menu Ideas

Summer evening Asparagus, Parma Ham and Nectarine Salad (p48),
Paella (p60) and Passionate Pavlova (p79).

Cook ahead Roasted Vegetable Bruschetta (p69), Chicken and Duck Terrine (p64)
and Baked Lemon and Sultana Cheesecake (p78).

Autumn evening Leek and Potato Soup (p50), Porcupine Meatballs in Red Wine Sauce (p59)
and Apple Strudel (p82).

Spicy supper Hot and Sour Seafood Soup (p51), Thai Red Chicken Curry (p72)
and Mango Fool (p76).

Get family and friends together and
create a special occasion

Asparagus, Parma Ham and Nectarine Salad

Pan frying the nectarines adds an extra dimension to this salad but, if it's easier, you can just leave them raw.

Serves 6

225 g (8 oz) asparagus tips
150 g (5½ oz) mixed baby salad leaves
6 slices Parma ham, roughly torn
20 g (¾ oz) Parmesan cheese shavings
low fat cooking spray
6 ripe nectarines, stoned and sliced into wedges

For the dressing
3 tablespoons balsamic vinegar
3 tablespoons clear honey
1½ teaspoons wholegrain mustard
salt and freshly ground black pepper

2 **POINTS** values per serving
13½ **POINTS** values per recipe

C 124 **calories** per serving

Takes **12 minutes** to prepare,
3 minutes to cook

✱ not recommended

1 Bring a pan of water to the boil and cook the asparagus tips for 3 minutes or until just tender. Drain and refresh in cold water to stop the cooking process.

2 Arrange the salad leaves on a large platter or shallow serving dish and top with the asparagus, Parma ham and Parmesan shavings.

3 Whisk the dressing ingredients together and set aside.

4 When ready to serve, heat a non stick frying pan, lightly coat with the cooking spray, add the nectarine wedges and fry for about 2 minutes until lightly caramelised. You will need to do this in two batches.

5 Scatter the nectarines over the salad, and drizzle on the dressing just before serving.

Leek and Potato Soup

This soup is delicious, filling and so simple to make. It freezes well, so why not make plenty of it so you can eat some now and save the rest for later.

Serves 6

1 tablespoon low fat spread

1 large onion, chopped finely

500 g (1lb 2 oz) leeks, chopped finely

500 g (1lb 2 oz) floury potatoes, peeled and chopped

3 tablespoons chopped fresh parsley, plus a few sprigs, to garnish

1 litre (1¾ pints) hot vegetable stock

300 ml (½ pint) skimmed milk

salt and freshly ground black pepper

1 Melt the low fat spread in a large, lidded, non stick saucepan and gently sauté the onion and leeks until soft, about 10 minutes.

2 Add the potatoes, parsley and hot stock and bring to the boil. Cover and reduce the heat. Simmer gently for about 20 minutes, or until the vegetables are tender and the potatoes are beginning to break down.

3 Add the milk to the saucepan and reheat gently. Season to taste and then ladle the soup into warmed bowls. Serve, garnished with parsley sprigs.

1½ *POINTS* values per serving
7½ **POINTS** values per recipe

C 122 calories per serving

Takes **15 minutes** to prepare, **35 minutes** to cook

V

✱ recommended

Tip If you prefer, liquidise the soup using a blender or hand held blender to make it extra smooth.

Variation Just use onions instead of leeks if you like – the soup will still be delicious. The *POINTS* values will remain the same.

Hot and Sour Seafood Soup

An unusual soup with a refreshing flavour that everyone will love.

Serves 4

500 ml (18 fl oz) chicken stock
1 teaspoon chilli paste (see Tip)
2 sticks of lemon grass, split
  lengthways
2.5 cm (1 inch) fresh root ginger,
  chopped roughly
1 shallot, chopped
1 teaspoon fish sauce

1 tablespoon lime juice
3 large tomatoes, skinned and
  chopped
6 kaffir lime leaves, torn (optional)
200 g (7 oz) mixed frozen seafood,
  defrosted
8 button mushrooms, quartered
1 tablespoon chopped fresh
  coriander, to garnish

1 Put the chicken stock in a pan with the chilli paste, stir and bring to a simmer.

2 Add the lemon grass, ginger, shallot, fish sauce, lime juice, tomatoes and kaffir lime leaves, if using. Mix well and bring to the boil. If you have time, leave this mixture to cool for an hour or so to allow the flavours to develop.

3 Sieve the soup to remove the aromatics. Reheat and add the seafood and mushrooms. Simmer for 2 minutes.

4 Serve in warmed bowls with the coriander sprinkled on top.

½ *POINTS* value per serving
2½ *POINTS* values per recipe

C 69 **calories** per serving

Takes **10 minutes** to prepare,
10 minutes to cook + cooling

* recommended at the end of step 2,
i.e. without the seafood

Tip This soup has quite a kick. If you're wary of the heat from the chilli paste, add ½ teaspoon to start with, then taste just before adding the seafood and add more if required.

Chicken Liver Pâté

Try this deliciously smooth pâté spread on crisp Melba toast (1 *POINTS* value for 6) as a starter. Alternatively, serve with zero *POINTS* value pickled cornichons (little gherkins) or silverskin onions as a light lunch.

Serves 4

250 g (9 oz) chicken livers, defrosted if frozen, rinsed

100 ml (3½ fl oz) skimmed milk

2 teaspoons low fat spread

1 small garlic clove, crushed

1 tablespoon chopped fresh thyme plus a few sprigs to garnish

2 tablespoons brandy

200 g (7 oz) low fat soft cheese

salt and freshly ground black pepper

1 Soak the chicken livers in the milk for 30 minutes to remove any bitterness, then discard the milk and pat the livers dry on kitchen paper.

2 Heat a non stick frying pan over a moderate heat. Melt the low fat spread in the pan, then add the chicken livers and stir fry for 3 minutes until browned on the outside but still slightly pink in the centre. Add the garlic, chopped thyme and some seasoning and cook for 30 seconds.

3 Remove the pan from the heat, add the brandy and stir to release any flavoursome bits from the base of the pan.

4 Tip the contents of the pan into a food processor, add the soft cheese and process in short bursts until smooth. Press the mixture through a sieve, then taste and adjust the seasoning if necessary.

5 Divide the pâté between four ramekins, garnish each with a sprig of thyme, cover and chill for at least 2 hours before serving.

Tip Sieving the pâté mixture gives it a smooth and creamy texture.

 2½ *POINTS* values per serving
11 POINTS values per recipe

C 109 **calories** per serving

Takes 5 **minutes** to prepare, 5 **minutes** to cook + 30 **minutes** soaking + 2 **hours** chilling

✱ recommended

Smoked Salmon Pinwheels with Roasted Asparagus

English asparagus has a relatively short season, May to June, but it's worth looking out for.

Serves 4

200 g (7 oz) asparagus tips
2 tablespoons balsamic vinegar
200 g (7 oz) thinly sliced smoked salmon
100 g (3½ oz) low fat soft cheese
salt and freshly ground black pepper
1 lemon, cut into wedges, to serve

1 Preheat the oven to Gas Mark 6/200ºC/fan oven 180ºC. Place the asparagus in a shallow roasting tray.

2 Drizzle over the balsamic vinegar and season, then roast in the oven for 5 minutes until just tender.

3 Lay a strip of the smoked salmon on a work surface and spread with a little soft cheese. Place three to four asparagus tips at one end of the strip and roll them up until they are enclosed in the salmon.

4 Place on a serving plate and repeat with the other salmon slices and asparagus. Serve scattered with ground black pepper and with lemon wedges to squeeze over.

2 POINTS values per serving
7 POINTS values per recipe

C **118 calories** per serving

Takes **5 minutes** to prepare, **5 minutes** to cook

✱ not recommended

Beef Wellington

Tender beef fillet wrapped in filo pastry with a quick mushroom pâté makes an impressive dinner party main course. Serve with steamed green beans, for no additional **POINTS** values.

Serves 4

400 g (14 oz) beef fillet
low fat cooking spray
200 g (7 oz) mushrooms, chopped finely
2 shallots, chopped finely
150 g (5½ oz) low fat soft cheese
1 tablespoon freshly chopped tarragon
12 x 15 g sheets filo pastry
salt and freshly ground black pepper

5½ **POINTS** values per serving
23 **POINTS** values per recipe

C 341 calories per serving

Takes **30 minutes** to prepare,
10 minutes to cook

✱ recommended

1 Preheat the oven to Gas Mark 7/220°C/fan oven 200°C.

2 Cut the beef into four equal portions and season. Lightly coat a non stick frying pan with the cooking spray and heat until hot. Add the meat and cook for 3–4 minutes until browned all over. Remove from the pan and set aside.

3 Spray the pan again with the cooking spray and add the mushrooms and shallots. Cook, stirring, for 10 minutes over a medium heat until the mushroom juices have been released and evaporated.

4 Place the soft cheese in a bowl and beat until smooth. Add the mushroom mixture and tarragon and mix well.

5 Lightly coat a baking tray with the cooking spray.

6 Lay one sheet of filo pastry on a board and spray with the cooking spray. Add another sheet and spray that, topping with a final sheet. Place a piece of beef in the middle of the sheets, spoon on a quarter of the mushroom mixture and wrap up. You can either do this neatly, as you would wrap a parcel, or bring up the sides and scrunch the top, making sure you seal in the contents. Carefully place on the baking tray and spray with the cooking spray. Repeat to make four parcels.

7 Bake the parcels for 10 minutes until the pastry is golden and crispy.

Tip You can freeze this dish (if the pastry was originally frozen, it can only be frozen once the pastry has been cooked). Bake, cool and wrap in foil. Defrost overnight in the fridge before reheating in an oven preheated to Gas Mark 6/200˚C/fan oven 180˚C for 10 minutes until piping hot.

Pesto Roast Peppers

These roast peppers, served with a zero **POINTS** value crunchy salad per person, make a wonderful starter. They are delicious eaten hot or cold.

Serves 4

4 red peppers, de-seeded and halved
3 spring onions, sliced
1 courgette, sliced
1 carrot, peeled and diced
2 tomatoes, diced
1 garlic clove, sliced
30 g (1¼ oz) pesto
salt and freshly ground black pepper
fresh basil leaves, torn, to garnish

1 **POINTS** value per serving
3 **POINTS** values per recipe

C 110 calories per serving

Takes **15 minutes** to prepare,
45–50 minutes to cook

V

✱ not recommended

1 Preheat the oven to Gas Mark 6/200°C/fan oven 180°C.

2 Place the pepper halves in a roasting tin, skin side down.

3 Place the remaining ingredients except the basil in a bowl and mix well to coat everything with the pesto.

4 Spoon the vegetable mixture into the peppers and bake for 45–50 minutes until the vegetables are soft.

5 Garnish with the basil. Serve two roasted pepper halves per person.

Variation Try topping the peppers, after 20 minutes of cooking, with 50 g (1¾ oz) of grated mozzarella light and then returning them to the oven for the remaining 25–30 minutes. The **POINTS** values will be 1½ per serving.

Moroccan Stew with Couscous

Serves 4

1 large onion, chopped
1 carrot, peeled and sliced thinly
2 teaspoons garlic purée
1 tablespoon ginger purée or freshly grated root
  ginger (optional)
1 large green chilli, de-seeded and chopped
2 teaspoons olive oil
1 teaspoon ground cumin
2 teaspoons ground coriander
1 teaspoon ground paprika
¼ teaspoon ground cinnamon
a good pinch of dried saffron strands or
  ¼ teaspoon turmeric (optional)
400 g can chopped tomatoes
1 courgette, chopped
400 g can chick peas, drained and liquid reserved
salt and freshly ground black pepper

For the couscous

200 g (7 oz) dried couscous
400 ml (14 fl oz) boiling water
2 tablespoons chopped fresh parsley
1 tablespoon chopped fresh dill or coriander

4½ *POINTS* values per serving
17½ *POINTS* values per recipe

C 350 calories per serving

Takes **15 minutes** to prepare,
20 minutes to cook

V

✱ recommended, freeze stew and couscous separately

1 First, start preparing the couscous. Put the couscous in a large bowl and pour over the boiling water. Season. Stir well and allow to cool, stirring occasionally with a fork to separate the grains.

2 For the stew, put the onion, carrot, garlic purée, ginger (if using) and chilli into a large, lidded, non stick saucepan with the oil and 4 tablespoons of water. Heat this mixture until it starts to sizzle, and then cover the pan and simmer for 10 minutes.

3 Remove the cover and stir in the cumin, coriander, paprika, cinnamon and saffron or turmeric, if using. Cook for 1 minute.

4 Add the canned tomatoes, courgette, chick peas with the reserved liquid and seasoning. Bring the pan to the boil and simmer for about 5 minutes until the courgette is tender.

5 Meanwhile, cover the couscous and reheat it in the microwave on High for 5 minutes. Alternatively, preheat the oven to Gas Mark 4/ 180°C/fan oven 160°C, place the couscous in an ovenproof dish, covered with foil, and heat for 10 minutes. When the couscous is piping hot, stir in the chopped herbs.

6 Serve the couscous with the stew spooned on top.

Porcupine Meatballs in Red Wine Sauce

These meatballs, made with rice, are inspired by a New Zealand dish. The rice puffs up as it cooks and sticks out of the meatballs giving them their spiky appearance, hence the name.

Serves 6

low fat cooking spray
1 onion, chopped finely
2 garlic cloves, crushed
400 g (14 oz) extra lean beef mince
150 g (5½ oz) dried long grain rice
a small bunch of fresh thyme, woody stems removed, leaves chopped, plus extra to garnish
2 carrots, peeled and diced finely
100 ml (3½ fl oz) red wine
400 g can chopped tomatoes
1 tablespoon Worcestershire sauce
300 ml (½ pint) stock
salt and freshly ground black pepper

4 POINTS values per serving
23 POINTS values per recipe

C **210 calories** per serving

Takes **30 minutes** to prepare, **30 minutes** to cook

✱ not recommended

1 Heat a large, lidded, non stick frying pan, spray with the cooking spray and then stir fry the onion and garlic for 5 minutes, or until softened, adding a little water if necessary to stop them sticking.

2 Take off the heat and place the onion and garlic in a large bowl with the mince, rice, thyme, carrots and seasoning and mix. Roll into 30 ping pong sized balls, squashing the mixture together with your hands.

3 In the same frying pan, brown the meatballs on all sides. Add all the remaining ingredients, bring to the boil and then cover and simmer for 30 minutes on a low heat. Serve garnished with the reserved thyme.

Paella

The name 'paella' actually refers to the large, flat cooking pan in which this famous Spanish fish recipe is cooked. It's one of the great dishes of the world.

Serves 6

a pinch of saffron strands
1.2 litres (2 pints) hot fish or chicken stock
low fat cooking spray
2 garlic cloves, crushed
a bunch of spring onions, chopped finely
1 red pepper, de-seeded and chopped
350 g (12 oz) dried arborio risotto rice
225 g (8 oz) squid rings
350 g (12 oz) cooked prawns in shells
450 g (1 lb) fresh mussels, scrubbed
2 tablespoons chopped fresh parsley
1 bay leaf
125 ml (4 fl oz) dry white wine
1 tablespoon lemon juice
50 g (1¾ oz) frozen petit pois or garden peas
salt and freshly ground black pepper
lemon wedges and chopped fresh parsley,
  to garnish

5 *POINTS* values per serving
29½ *POINTS* values per recipe

C 345 calories per serving

Takes **20 minutes** to prepare,
45 minutes to cook

✱ recommended

1 Add the saffron strands to the hot stock and let them infuse for 10–15 minutes.

2 Heat a wok or large non stick frying pan and spray it with the cooking spray. Add the garlic, spring onions and red pepper. Sauté them for about 5 minutes until softened.

3 Add the rice to the wok or frying pan and sauté for 1 minute. Pour in the saffron infused hot stock and bring to the boil. Reduce the heat and simmer for 10 minutes.

4 Add all the remaining ingredients, apart from the garnish, and stir well. Cook gently, uncovered, for about 20 minutes, stirring occasionally, until the liquid has been absorbed and the rice is tender. Add a little extra liquid if it has all been absorbed before the rice is cooked.

5 Discard the bay leaf and any mussels that have not opened during cooking. Season well and then serve, garnished with lemon wedges and parsley.

Tip When preparing fresh mussels, be sure to discard any that are damaged, or remain open when tapped.

Variation To make a chicken paella, replace the squid and mussels with 350 g (12 oz) of chopped, cooked chicken 10 minutes before the end of the cooking time. The *POINTS* values per serving will be 5½.

Wild Mushroom Risotto

Wild mushrooms give this risotto a rich flavour.

Serves 4

20 g packet of dried mushrooms, e.g. porcini
150 ml (¼ pint) boiling water
low fat cooking spray
1 onion, chopped finely
2 garlic cloves, crushed
350 g (12 oz) dried arborio risotto rice
100 ml (3½ fl oz) white wine
200 g (7 oz) button mushrooms, sliced
1.2 litres (2 pints) hot vegetable stock
a small bunch of fresh parsley, chopped
salt and freshly ground black pepper
50 g (1¾ oz) Parmesan cheese, grated finely,
 to serve

1 Place the dried mushrooms in a measuring jug and add the boiling water. Soak for 25 minutes.

2 Heat a large saucepan, spray with the cooking spray and stir fry the onion and garlic until softened, adding a little water if necessary to stop them sticking.

3 Add the rice and stir to mix well, then add the wine. Drain the reconstituted mushrooms, reserving the soaking liquid, and chop into small pieces. Strain the soaking liquid through a fine mesh sieve or piece of muslin and add to the risotto with the reconstituted and fresh mushrooms.

4 Add the stock in small quantities, cooking and stirring frequently until all of it has been absorbed.

5 Check the seasoning and stir in the parsley. Serve with the Parmesan cheese sprinkled over the top.

6 *POINTS* values per serving
24½ POINTS values per recipe

C **418 calories** per serving

Takes **30 minutes** to prepare,
30 minutes to cook

V

✱ not recommended

Tip When cooking risotto rice, add the stock a ladleful at a time, making sure each quantity has been absorbed before adding more.

Asian Tuna Parcels

The ginger, garlic and spring onions release a wonderful scent when the parcel is opened. Serve with 150 g (5½ oz) portion of cooked brown rice per person, for 3 additional **POINTS** values per serving.

Serves 4

6 **spring onions, sliced**
2 **garlic cloves, sliced thinly**
5 cm (2 inch) **fresh root ginger, cut into matchsticks**
4 **heads pak choi**
4 x 150 g (5½ oz) **fresh tuna steaks**
4 **tablespoons dark soy sauce**

1 Preheat the oven to Gas Mark 6/200°C/fan oven 180°C.

2 Line a large roasting tin with a sheet of foil, big enough to double back over the roasting tin. Scatter half the spring onions, garlic and ginger over the base of the lined tin.

3 Cut each head of pak choi into quarters through the root then add to the roasting tin.

4 Place the tuna steaks on top of the pak choi and scatter with the rest of the spring onions, garlic and ginger. Drizzle the soy sauce all over then crimp the edges of the foil tightly to make a large parcel.

5 Bake in the oven for 12 minutes, then carefully undo the foil and serve the tuna on the bed of pak choi.

2½ **POINTS** values per serving
9½ **POINTS** values per recipe

C 200 **calories** per serving

Takes 8 **minutes** to prepare,
12 **minutes** to cook

* not recommended

Chicken and Duck Terrine

Although this is a terrine, it makes a great dinner party main course when served with a zero **POINTS** value salad and 110 g (4 oz) hot new potatoes per person, for a **POINTS** value of 1 per serving. It's not difficult and the end result is impressive.

Serves 8

2 x 150 g (5½ oz) skinless boneless chicken breasts
2 x 150 g (5½ oz) skinless boneless duck breasts
100 ml (3½ fl oz) port
250 g (9 oz) lean pork mince
2 tablespoons chopped fresh tarragon
zest of a small orange
1 egg
1 egg white
25 g (1 oz) green or black olives in brine, drained and chopped
12 rashers smoked streaky bacon
125 g (4½ oz) whole cooked sweet peppers from a jar, drained and cut into strips
low fat cooking spray
salt and freshly ground black pepper

5½ **POINTS** values per serving
43 **POINTS** values per recipe

C 287 calories per serving

Takes **30 minutes** to prepare,
1½ **hours** to cook + overnight chilling

✱ recommended

1 Cut the chicken breasts and one of the duck breasts into four equal strips. Place in a non metallic dish and marinate in the port for 10 minutes.

2 Cut the remaining duck breast into small pieces. Place in a bowl with the pork mince, tarragon, orange zest, eggs and olives. Mix well and season.

3 Preheat the oven to Gas Mark 2/150ºC/fan oven 130ºC. Line a 900 g (2 lb) loaf tin with the bacon rashers, ensuring they meet and overlap on the base and overhang the edges enough to cover the contents. You don't need to cover the ends of the tin.

4 Drain the chicken and duck breasts, pouring any excess marinade into the pork mixture and mixing well. Spoon half the pork mixture into the tin. Lay the chicken and duck pieces on top, pressing down to level the surface. Arrange the strips of pepper evenly over the surface and spread with the remaining pork mixture.

5 Fold the overhanging bacon rashers over the top. Spray some foil with the cooking spray and use to cover the loaf tin, sprayed side down. Place on a baking tray and bake for 1½ hours.

6 Remove from the oven and pour off about half the liquid in the tin around the terrine. Cool, then chill overnight with weights (use cans) on top to press it down. Serve cold or reheat in a microwave until piping hot.

Tips Store in the fridge, wrapped in cling film for up to 5 days or wrap and freeze. Individual portions can be used for a lunchbox.

Duck breasts are expensive so you could replace them with chicken breasts, for 5 **POINTS** values per serving, although the flavour will not be quite so gamey.

Moroccan Lamb Tagine

This fragrant Moroccan lamb stew is slow cooked with aromatic spices to give a delicious, mellow flavour.

Serves 4

low fat cooking spray
450 g (1 lb) lean lamb leg steak, cubed
1 large onion, chopped
1 teaspoon ground cinnamon
1 teaspoon ground coriander
1 teaspoon ground ginger
600 ml (1 pint) hot lamb stock
100 g (3½ oz) ready to eat dried apricots
100 g (3½ oz) dried couscous
175 ml (6 fl oz) boiling water
salt and freshly ground black pepper
fresh coriander sprigs, to garnish

4½ *POINTS* values per serving
18 *POINTS* values per recipe

C 370 calories per serving

Takes **20 minutes** to prepare,
1 hour 40 minutes to cook

* recommended

1 Heat a large, lidded, heavy based saucepan and spray with the cooking spray. Add the lamb, a handful at a time, until it is browned on all sides.

2 Add the onion and cook for 2–3 minutes, and then add the cinnamon, coriander and ginger. Cook for another 2 minutes.

3 Pour in the stock and bring to the boil. Reduce the heat, cover and simmer for about 1¼ hours until the meat is very tender.

4 Add the apricots to the stew and cook, uncovered, for another 15–20 minutes, so that the liquid reduces.

5 Meanwhile, in a bowl, add the couscous and cover with the boiling water. Stir briefly and cover with a plate. Leave to stand for 7 minutes.

6 Season the tagine and serve it with the couscous, garnished with fresh coriander sprigs.

Braised Pheasant with Port and Mushrooms

This autumnal dish is delicious served with mashed root vegetables such as carrots, swede and turnips or a mixture of these and some meltingly soft braised red cabbage.

Serves 4

400 g (14 oz) skinless pheasant breast fillets, cut into bite size pieces

100 ml (3½ fl oz) port

1 teaspoon dried oregano or Mediterranean herbs

1 large onion, sliced

2 cloves garlic, crushed

450 g (1 lb) chestnut or other mushrooms, cleaned and halved

600 ml (1 pint) chicken stock

salt and freshly ground black pepper

1 Place the pheasant breasts in a shallow bowl and pour over the port and herbs, then leave to marinate for at least 2 hours, but overnight if possible.

2 Drain the meat thoroughly, reserving the marinade.

3 Heat a large, lidded, non stick pan or casserole, season the pheasant breasts, then dry fry until browned all over.

4 Add the onion and garlic and cook for 5 minutes, or until softened, then add the mushrooms and seasoning. Add the reserved marinade and scrape up any bits stuck on the bottom of the pan, then add the stock and bring to the boil.

5 Simmer gently for 35 minutes, covered, then remove the lid and boil rapidly for 10 minutes to reduce the sauce. Check the seasoning and serve.

4½ *POINTS* values per serving
17½ **POINTS** values per recipe

C **292 calories** per serving

Takes **35 minutes** to prepare + at least **2 hours** marinating, **45 minutes** to cook

✱ recommended

Roasted Vegetable Bruschetta

A colourful and tasty starter that will get your taste buds going.

Serves 8

½ red onion, cut into chunks

8 small button mushrooms, halved

½ yellow pepper, de-seeded and sliced thinly

1 baby courgette, sliced thinly

low fat cooking spray

150 g (5½ oz) baguette

1 garlic clove, halved

8 cherry tomatoes

8 basil leaves

1 Preheat the oven to Gas Mark 5/190°C/fan oven 170°C. Place the onion, mushrooms, pepper and courgette in a roasting tin and spray with the cooking spray. Roast in the oven for 30 minutes, shaking the vegetables halfway through. You can do all this several hours in advance.

2 To serve, diagonally cut the baguette into eight slices. Use a hot griddle or ridged pan to brown the slices on both sides for a chargrilled effect. Alternatively, toast them under a hot grill.

3 Rub the cut side of the garlic clove over the hot bruschetta slices to flavour the bread. Squash a tomato on to each slice of bruschetta, then top with a basil leaf and the roasted vegetables.

½ *POINTS* value per serving
6 *POINTS* values per recipe

C 55 calories per serving

Takes 15 minutes to prepare, 30 minutes to cook

V

✱ not recommended

Tip This is best served within an hour if you don't want the vegetables to make the bread soggy.

Salmon en Croute

Fresh salmon fillets wrapped and baked in sheets of filo pastry make a really special meal. Serve with fresh asparagus or fine green beans and 100 g (3½ oz) new potatoes per person, for 1 extra **POINTS** value per serving.

Serves 4

low fat cooking spray
6 x 15 g sheets filo pastry, defrosted if frozen
2 tablespoons plain white flour
4 x 140 g (5 oz) fresh salmon fillets
  (do not use steaks)
60 g (2 oz) low fat soft cheese with garlic
  and herbs
finely grated zest of a lemon
4 teaspoons chopped fresh dill or parsley
salt and freshly ground black pepper

6½ **POINTS** values per serving
26 **POINTS** values per recipe

C 395 calories per serving

Takes **20 minutes** to prepare,
30–35 minutes to cook

✻ recommended

1 Preheat the oven to Gas Mark 4/180°C/fan oven 160°C. Lightly spray a baking sheet with the cooking spray.

2 Take a sheet of filo pastry, spray it with the cooking spray and then lay another sheet on top. Spray the second sheet in the same way, and then place a third sheet on top and spray yet again. Cut this stack in half widthways. Repeat the process with the remaining three sheets to give you four piles of filo pastry.

3 Sprinkle the flour onto a plate and season. Rinse the salmon fillets and pat them dry with kitchen paper. Check that there are no bones in them and then dip them in the flour, patting off any excess.

4 Place a piece of floured fish in the middle of each pile of pastry and then spoon an equal amount of soft cheese on top of each fillet. Spread it over the surface and sprinkle the lemon zest and herbs on top. Season lightly.

5 Fold the filo pastry over the fillets to make parcels, tucking in the ends. Lift the parcels onto the baking sheet and lightly spray them with the cooking spray. Bake in the oven for 30–35 minutes, until the pastry is golden.

Variation Try using trout fillets or sea bass. The **POINTS** values will be 4 and 4½ per serving respectively.

Thai Red Chicken Curry

Making your own Thai curry paste is surprisingly easy and doesn't take long.

Serves 4

For the red curry paste
½ red onion, chopped roughly
1 red chilli, de-seeded and sliced
1 small stick lemongrass, sliced thinly
grated zest and juice of ½ a lime
2.5 cm (1 inch) fresh root ginger, sliced
1 garlic clove
1 tablespoon Thai fish sauce

For the curry
4 dried Kaffir lime leaves (optional)
100 ml (3½ fl oz) boiling water
150 g (5½ oz) baby corn, sliced
150 g (5½ oz) sugar snap peas
low fat cooking spray
350 g (12 oz) skinless boneless chicken
  breast, diced
6 spring onions, cut into thirds
200 ml (7 fl oz) reduced fat coconut milk
200 ml (7 fl oz) chicken stock
1 teaspoon light soft brown sugar
110 g (4 oz) cherry tomatoes, halved
chopped fresh coriander, to garnish

3 POINTS values per serving
11½ POINTS values per recipe

C **194 calories** per serving

Takes **30 minutes**

* recommended

1 Place the curry paste ingredients in a food processor or use a hand held blender and blend until finely chopped.

2 Soak the lime leaves (if using) in boiling water for 5 minutes and then cut into fine shreds.

3 Bring a pan of water to the boil, add the baby corn and sugar snaps and cook for 3 minutes then drain and set aside.

4 Heat a wok or large non stick frying pan and spray with the cooking spray. Stir fry the chicken and spring onions for 3 minutes, then add the curry paste and fry for 1 minute.

5 Blend in the coconut milk and chicken stock then add the shredded lime leaves (if using), sugar and blanched vegetables. Simmer gently for 3 minutes, then add the cherry tomatoes and cook for 2 minutes before ladling into warmed bowls. Garnish with chopped coriander.

Tip Dried Kaffir lime leaves are available in the spice section of most supermarkets. They add a wonderful perfumed fragrance to Thai food.

Variations To make green Thai curry paste, substitute a green chilli for the red, regular onion in place of the red onion and add 2 tablespoons of freshly chopped coriander. The **POINTS** values will remain the same.

V For a vegetarian Thai curry, use light soy sauce in the curry paste instead of fish sauce, vegetable stock rather than chicken and then add 350 g (12 oz) cooked diced sweet potato in place of the chicken, adding it at step 5. The **POINTS** values will be reduced to 2½ per serving.

Braised Pork with Apricots

For easy entertaining, this dish can be made ahead then gently reheated before serving.

Serves 6

800 g (1 lb 11 oz) pork fillet, visible fat removed and cut into 1 cm (½ inch) slices
low fat cooking spray
425 ml (15 fl oz) chicken stock
150 ml (¼ pint) white wine
175 g (6 oz) dried apricots, halved
½ teaspoon mixed spice
1 tablespoon dark soy sauce
4 teaspoons clear honey
2 tablespoons cornflour
2 tablespoons freshly chopped parsley
salt and freshly ground black pepper

1 Pat the slices of pork fillet dry on kitchen paper, then season lightly. Heat a non stick frying pan, spray with the cooking spray then brown one third of the pork, cooking for 1½ minutes on each side.

2 When the first batch of pork is done, transfer to a flameproof casserole, swirl one third of the stock around the frying pan to release the flavour and pour into the casserole.

3 Place the frying pan back on the heat, coat with a little more cooking spray, then brown the next batch and cook in the same way. Repeat until all the pork is cooked.

4 Pour the white wine into the frying pan and bring to the boil, scraping the bottom of the pan with a spoon to released any caramelised juices.

5 Tip the wine into the casserole and stir in the apricots, mixed spice, soy sauce and honey. Bring to a simmer, cover and cook gently for 20 minutes.

6 Mix the cornflour with 1 tablespoon of cold water and add to the casserole, stirring until thickened, then add the parsley and seasoning to taste just before serving.

5½ **POINTS** values per serving
32 POINTS values per recipe

C **311 calories** per serving

Takes **10 minutes** to prepare, **30 minutes** to cook

* recommended

Lemon and Blueberry Charlottes

A deliciously creamy dessert that's perfect for serving to friends as it looks so special. Serve straightaway, or cover and chill until ready to serve.

Serves 4

10 sponge fingers
zest and juice of ½ a lemon
100 g (3½ oz) low fat soft cheese
135 g pot low fat custard
100 g (3½ oz) blueberries, reserving some for the top
1 teaspoon caster sugar for dusting

1 Cut each sponge finger lengthways and then in half to make four short pieces. Mix 1 tablespoon of lemon juice with 1 tablespoon of water and brush this all over the sponge fingers. Arrange ten pieces of sponge finger upright around the sides of four ramekins.

2 Whisk the rest of the lemon juice and the zest into the soft cheese and custard, then fold in all but the reserved blueberries. Spoon into the ramekins, inside the lining of sponge fingers.

3 Garnish with the reserved blueberries, a little extra lemon zest and a sprinkling of caster sugar if you like.

2 POINTS values per serving
8½ POINTS values per recipe

C **138 calories** per serving

Takes **10 minutes**

V

***** not recommended

Mango Fool

A light and fresh dessert that will help to clear the palate after a rich or spicy meal.

Serves 4

2 ripe mangoes
100 g (3½ oz) low fat crème fraîche
90 g (3¼ oz) low fat natural yogurt
8 wafer thin biscuits, to serve

3½ *POINTS* values per serving
13 *POINTS* values per recipe

C   **150 calories** per serving

Takes **5 minutes**

V

✱   not recommended

1   Peel the mangoes and cut off the flesh from the stone. Place half the fruit in a food processor and blend until smooth. Chop the remaining fruit.

2   Beat together the crème fraîche and yogurt and stir in the puréed mango.

3   Divide the creamy mango mixture between four ramekins or glasses. Top with the chopped mango and chill until ready to serve. Serve with the wafer thin biscuits, for dipping.

Baked Lemon and Sultana Cheesecake

This baked cheesecake is absolutely sensational with the sultanas adding a natural sweetness.

Serves 8

175 g (6 oz) reduced fat digestive biscuits, crushed
75 g (2¾ oz) low fat spread, melted
350 g (12 oz) low fat plain cottage cheese
50 g (1¾ oz) caster sugar
finely grated zest and juice of 2 lemons
3 eggs
150 g (5½ oz) half fat crème fraîche
½ teaspoon ground cinnamon
50 g (1¾ oz) sultanas
1 teaspoon icing sugar, to serve

5 *POINTS* values per serving
41½ *POINTS* values per recipe

C 258 calories per serving

Takes **25 minutes** to prepare,
1¼ hours to bake + **2 hours** cooling

V

✱ recommended

1 Mix the crushed biscuits with the low fat spread and press over the base of a 20 cm (8 inch) loose bottomed springform tin.

2 Preheat the oven to Gas Mark 3/160ºC/fan oven 140ºC.

3 Push the cottage cheese through a sieve and then beat in the caster sugar, lemon zest and juice, eggs, crème fraîche, cinnamon and sultanas.

4 Spoon the cheese mixture over the biscuit base and bake for 1¼ hours.

5 Open the oven door and allow the cheesecake to cool in the oven for about 2 hours.

6 Carefully remove the cheesecake from the tin and place it on a serving plate. Dust the top with the icing sugar to serve.

Tip Crush the biscuits by putting them in a polythene bag and bashing them with a rolling pin, alternatively use a food processor.

Passionate Pavlova

This meringue-based dessert makes a big, bold and beautiful party extravaganza to be proud of.

Serves 6

4 egg whites
150 g (5½ oz) caster sugar

For the topping
100 g (3½ oz) Quark
400 g (14 oz) very low fat fromage frais
50 g (1¾ oz) icing sugar, plus extra for dusting
4 passion fruit, seeds and juice scooped out of the shells
2 ripe nectarines, stoned and cut into wedges
450 g (1 lb) strawberries, hulled and sliced

3 *POINTS* values per serving
19 *POINTS* values per recipe

C 220 calories per serving

Takes **20 minutes** to prepare,
1 hours to bake + **2–3 hours** cooling

V

✳ not recommended

1 Preheat the oven to Gas Mark ½/120°C/fan oven 100°C. In a clean, grease free bowl and with an electric whisk, whisk the egg whites until they are stiff and dry. Whisk in half the caster sugar, then add the other half and whisk again until stiff and glossy.

2 Line a baking sheet with non stick baking parchment, put a 20 cm (8 inch) dinner plate on top and draw round it. Remove the plate and spoon the meringue onto the baking parchment to cover the circle, building up the edge and swirling the meringue to make a large, slightly concave nest.

3 Bake for 1 hour. Open the oven door and leave to cool in the oven for 2–3 hours.

4 Carefully peel off the paper and place the meringue on a serving dish.

5 To decorate, beat together the Quark, fromage frais and icing sugar and spoon onto the pavlova. Top with the fruit and dust with icing sugar to serve.

Chocolate Roulade

Here is a low **POINTS** value version of this delectable French dessert, ideal for any special occasion.

Serves 8

low fat cooking spray
150 g (5½ oz) caster sugar
8 egg whites
a pinch of cream of tartar
50 g (1¾ oz) cocoa powder, plus extra for dusting
1½ teaspoons vanilla extract
mint sprigs, to serve

For the filling

200 g (7 oz) low fat natural yogurt
50 g (1¾ oz) white cooking chocolate, melted
1 tablespoon caster sugar
1 teaspoon vanilla extract
200 g (7 oz) fresh raspberries, a few reserved
  for decoration

3 **POINTS** values per serving
23½ **POINTS** values per recipe

C 165 calories per serving

Takes **20 minutes** to prepare,
30 minutes to cook + cooling

V

✱ not recommended

1 Preheat the oven to Gas Mark 4/180°C/fan oven 160°C. Spray a 33 x 23 cm (13 x 9-inch) Swiss roll tin with the cooking spray. Lay a large sheet of greaseproof baking parchment on the work surface and dust it evenly with 2 tablespoons of the caster sugar.

2 Place the egg whites in a bowl with the cream of tartar and whisk until they form soft peaks.

3 Add the remaining caster sugar a little at a time and continue to whisk until thick and glossy. Fold in the cocoa and vanilla extract very carefully, taking care not to knock out the air.

4 Scrape the mixture into the prepared baking tin, taking it right into the corners. Bake for 30 minutes until firm and springy to the touch.

5 Leave the roulade to cool in the tin, then turn out onto the greaseproof baking parchment.

6 To make the filling, mix together all the ingredients and then spread evenly over the unrolled roulade. Then roll up using the greaseproof baking parchment to help. Dust with the reserved cocoa powder and decorate with more fresh raspberries and mint sprigs to serve.

Apple Strudel

British-grown Bramley apples are a great seasonal ingredient. When combined with spices and dried fruit they make a delicious strudel filling. Serve with a 60 g (2 oz) scoop of low fat vanilla ice cream per person, for 1 additional **POINTS** value per serving.

Serves 6

750 g (1 lb 10 oz) cooking apples, peeled, cored and diced
zest and juice of ½ a lemon
1 teaspoon ground cinnamon
60 g (2 oz) soft light brown sugar
50 g (1¾ oz) sultanas
25 g (1 oz) fresh wholemeal breadcrumbs
4 x 45 g sheets frozen filo pastry, defrosted
25 g (1 oz) low fat spread, melted
low fat cooking spray
1 teaspoon icing sugar, for dusting

3 **POINTS** values per serving
17½ **POINTS** values per recipe

C 219 calories per serving

Takes **20 minutes** to prepare, **30 mintes** to cook

V

* recommended

1 Preheat the oven to Gas Mark 4/180°C/fan oven 160°C. In a mixing bowl, toss the diced apples with the lemon zest and juice, then mix in the cinnamon, sugar, sultanas and breadcrumbs. Set this aside.

2 Lay a clean tea towel flat on the work surface and place two sheets of filo pastry on it side by side, like the pages of a book, making sure that they overlap by 2.5 cm (1 inch). Brush lightly with the melted low fat spread then layer the remaining filo on top as before, but placing the pastry at right angles to the first two sheets, overlapping slightly. Brush with a little more low fat spread.

3 Heap the filling along the edge of the pastry nearest to you, leaving a gap of 5 cm (2 inches) at each end.

4 Lightly spray a baking tray with the cooking spray. Lifting the nearest edge of the tea towel up and away from you, roll the pastry tightly around the filling, tucking in the ends as you go so that the apple filling won't fall out. Lift up the strudel, still on the tea towel, then carefully tip it on to the baking tray, with the seam tucked underneath.

5 Brush with any leftover melted low fat spread and bake for 30 minutes until the pastry is golden and the apples in the filling feel tender when pierced with a skewer. Dust with the icing sugar before serving.

Tip Filo pastry can be rather delicate to handle, and has a tendency to dry out. Remove the plastic wrappings and unroll the filo pastry on to a piece of baking parchment. Dampen a clean tea towel then wring it out tightly and lay it on top of the filo to prevent it from drying out as you work.

Party! Party!

Menu Ideas

Oriental party Chicken Satay Skewers (p111), Thai Spring Rolls (p92) and Thai Fish Cakes with Sweet Chilli Dip (p107).

Teenage party Sausage Rolls (p102), Mini Pizzas (p88), Tortilla Chips and Dips (p103), Cheesy Chicken Goujons (p114) and Chocolate Brownie Cake (p115).

Drinks party Tapas Plates (p86), Spicy Nuts (p91) and Houmous with Pitta (p99).

Party food that is healthy – a good reason to celebrate

Tapas Plates

Spanish tapas typically consists of lots of little dishes. These are easily assembled and can be prepared in advance and then thrown together at the last minute.

Serves 4

110 g (4 oz) chorizo, cut into 12 pieces
4 slices Serrano ham

For the marinated olives

12 black olives in brine, drained, stoned
  and halved
1 teaspoon olive oil
1 tablespoon orange juice
½ teaspoon cumin seeds

For the marinated artichokes

400 g can artichokes in water, drained
zest and juice of a lemon
1 teaspoon dried oregano

For the dip

4 tablespoons virtually fat free fromage frais
1 garlic clove, crushed
1 tablespoon finely chopped parsley

---

3 *POINTS* values per serving
12 *POINTS* values per recipe

171 **calories** per serving

Takes **15 minutes** to prepare,
+ **1 hour** marinating

✳ not recommended

1 Combine all the ingredients for the marinated olives, cover and set aside for 1 hour.

2 Combine all the ingredients for the marinated artichokes, cover and set aside for 1 hour.

3 To make the dip, combine all the ingredients, cover and chill until required.

4 Heat a small, non stick frying pan and dry fry the chorizo pieces for 2–3 minutes until beginning to colour.

5 Place the tapas, including the chorizo and Serrano ham, on individual serving plates or bowls. Place the dip on the side for dipping and let people help themselves.

Tips You can marinate the olives and artichokes overnight in the fridge if preferred.

Buy your chorizo sausage at the deli counter instead of ready sliced, so that you can cut it into pieces.

Mini Pizzas

These are ideal as nibbles at a drinks party. There are two varieties and, as one is vegetarian, they are suitable for a mixed group of guests. They also make an unusual starter for a supper party.

Makes 16

1 heaped tablespoon flour, for dusting
100 g (3½ oz) pizza base mix
½ small onion, chopped very finely
1 garlic clove, crushed
200 g (7 oz) canned chopped tomatoes
½ teaspoon sugar
½ teaspoon dried oregano or basil
2 tablespoons tomato purée
125 g (4½ oz) mozzarella light cheese
40 g (1½ oz) wafer thin ham
2 small mushrooms, sliced very thinly
8 slices tomatoes, each approximately 5 mm
 (¼ inch) thick
16 small basil leaves

1 *POINTS* value per serving
16 *POINTS* values per recipe

C 50 calories per serving

Takes **30 minutes**

V tomato and mozzarella variety only

* recommended

1 Dust a flat work surface with the flour. Add 75 ml (3 fl oz) warm water to the pizza base mix or follow the instructions on the packet. Knead well for 5 minutes on the floured surface.

2 Roll out into a rough circle about 30 cm (12 inches) across. Use a 6 cm (2½ inch) biscuit cutter to cut 16 mini pizzas from the dough. For a more rustic look, divide the dough into 16 pieces and squash with the ball of your hand to form circles roughly 6 cm (2½ inches) across. Place these on to a non stick baking sheet and leave to stand in a warm place for about 10 minutes to allow the dough to rise.

3 Preheat the oven to Gas Mark 7/220°C/fan oven 200°C. Meanwhile, place the onion, garlic, canned tomatoes, sugar, herbs and tomato purée in a small saucepan. Mix well and bring to a simmer, and then cook for 10 minutes or until the mixture is thick enough to spread on the pizzas.

4 Cut eight thin slices from the mozzarella, which will be about two-thirds of the cheese. Grate or finely chop the remaining mozzarella.

5 Put a spoonful of the tomato sauce on each pizza and spread it close to the edges. Divide the ham and mushrooms between eight of the pizzas and top with the grated mozzarella. Put the eight tomato slices, topped with a slice of mozzarella, on the remaining eight pizzas.

6 Bake in the oven for 10 minutes or until golden and crisp. Serve warm, garnished with the basil leaves.

Tip This quantity of tomato sauce is enough for two batches of mini pizzas. Freeze any that is unused for another time.

Greek-style Lamb Kebabs

These kebabs are a cross between a burger and a sausage, so they should go down well with the family.

Serves 4

2 medium slices of white bread, crusts removed
450 g (1 lb) lean lamb mince
1 small onion, grated
1 teaspoon garlic purée
1 teaspoon dried oregano
1 teaspoon dried mint
½ teaspoon paprika
1 teaspoon salt
1 egg, beaten

1 Preheat the grill to medium and line the grill pan with foil.

2 Wet the bread under a running tap and squeeze out the excess water. Crumble into small pieces.

3 Using clean hands, mix together all the ingredients, including the breadcrumbs, and bind them well. Divide the mixture into 12 even parts and make each into a short sausage. Thread them on to metal skewers and place directly onto the grill pan.

4 Cook under a hot grill for 12–15 minutes, turning frequently to ensure even cooking.

6½ *POINTS* values per serving
26 POINTS values per recipe

C 265 calories per serving

Takes 30 minutes

✳ recommended

Tip Delicious served with tzatziki. Stir 1 tablespoon chopped fresh parsley, 1 tablespoon chopped fresh chives, ½ teaspoon Dijon mustard, 3 tablespoons chopped fresh mint, a 5 cm (2-inch) piece of cucumber, diced, and some pepper into 150 g (5½ oz) 0% fat Greek style yogurt. The *POINTS* values will be 1 per recipe.

Variation Thread tomato halves, pieces of green pepper and slices of courgettes between the lamb on the kebabs for a more substantial meal without adding any extra *POINTS* values.

Spicy Nuts

Delicious to nibble with a pre dinner drink and much more impressive than opening a packet.

Serves 8

1 teaspoon salt
¼ teaspoon artificial sweetener
½ teaspoon ground ginger
½ teaspoon ground coriander
½ teaspoon ground cinnamon
½ teaspoon ground cumin

½ teaspoon garam masala
100 g (3½ oz) cashew nuts
100 g (3½ oz) pecan nuts
50 g (1¾ oz) almonds
low fat cooking spray

1 Preheat the oven to Gas Mark 6/200°C/fan oven 180°C.

2 Mix together the salt, sweetener and all the spices. Add 1 tablespoon of water to make a paste.

3 Mix the nuts together in a bowl and add the paste. Mix really well to coat the nuts in the paste.

4 Spray a roasting tray with the cooking spray and pour on the nuts.

5 Cook in the oven for 10 minutes. Stir the nuts and then cook for a further 5 minutes. Remove from the oven and allow to cool on the tray.

3½ **POINTS** values per serving
27½ **POINTS** values per recipe

C 205 **calories** per serving

Takes **5 minutes** to prepare,
15 minutes to cook

V

✱ not recommended

Thai Spring Rolls

These spring rolls are light, tasty and so low in **POINTS** values – a far cry from the deep fried restaurant versions.

Makes 8

50 g packet (8 pancakes) rice flour pancakes for spring rolls
50 g (1¾ oz) fresh beansprouts
2 spring onions, sliced finely
½ red pepper, de-seeded and sliced very finely
2–3 Chinese leaves or Cos lettuce leaves, shredded finely
50 g (1¾ oz) cooked small prawns, defrosted if frozen
1 teaspoon seasoned rice vinegar or white wine vinegar
2 teaspoons Thai fish sauce or soy sauce
salt and freshly ground black pepper
4 tablespoons sweet chilli sauce, to serve

½ **POINTS** value per serving
4½ **POINTS** values per recipe

C 55 calories per serving

Takes **15 minutes**

✳ not recommended

1 First, prepare the rice flour pancakes. Take two clean tea towels, run them under the cold tap and wring them out. Spread one out on a worktop, lay the spring roll pancakes on top, and then cover them with the second damp tea towel. Leave for 1–2 minutes until the pancakes are soft and pliable.

2 Put all the vegetables and the prawns into a bowl, and add the rice vinegar or white wine vinegar and the fish sauce or soy sauce. Season and then toss everything together.

3 Place an equal amount of the vegetable and prawn filling down the centre of each pancake. Fold in the sides, and then roll up each pancake to enclose the filling.

4 Cover and chill the spring rolls until ready to serve. Serve chilled, accompanied by the sweet chilli sauce for dipping.

Tip For the spring roll pancakes, it's a good idea to check the packet instructions on preparation as individual brands may differ slightly.

Variations If you like, add a few raw sliced button mushrooms in step two, for the same **POINTS** value per serving.

V For a vegetarian alternative, omit the prawns and make sure that you use soy sauce, not fish sauce. The **POINTS** values will remain the same.

BBQ Chicken Drumsticks

These sweet and spicy chicken drumsticks can be cooked on a griddle or under the grill but they are best with that charred flavour you get from a BBQ.

Makes 12

12 x 47 g (1¾ oz) skinless chicken drumsticks

For the marinade
2 garlic cloves, crushed
2.5 cm (1-inch) fresh root ginger, grated
zest and juice of 2 oranges
1 small red chilli, de-seeded and chopped finely
2 tablespoons clear honey
2 tablespoons soy sauce
2 tablespoons tomato purée
2 teaspoons sesame oil

1 Mix all the marinade ingredients together into a paste. Put the drumsticks in a shallow dish, add the marinade and turn to coat. Leave to marinate in the fridge for at least 4 hours but preferably overnight.

2 Cook the drumsticks on a griddle, under the grill or on a hot BBQ for 7–8 minutes on each side until thoroughly cooked and golden brown.

1½ POINTS values per serving
18½ POINTS values per recipe

96 calories per serving

Takes **5 minutes** to prepare + at least **4 hours** marinating, **15 minutes** to cook

✱ not recommended

Variation For a quicker and more convenient marinade, use 6 tablespoons of ready-made barbecue sauce mixed with 2 tablespoons of water, for the same **POINTS** values per serving.

Marinated Prawns in Lettuce Boats

This simple summer buffet dish is quick and easy – the prawns just need time to marinate.

Makes 12

100 g (3½ oz) very low fat plain fromage frais
1 small garlic clove, crushed
1 teaspoon grated fresh root ginger
zest and juice of ½ a lemon
2 tablespoons freshly chopped parsley
2 tablespoons freshly chopped basil
300 g (10½ oz) cooked and peeled tiger prawns
2 Little Gem lettuces
salt and freshly ground black pepper

1 Stir the fromage frais together with the garlic, ginger and lemon zest and juice, then mix in the herbs and seasoning to taste.

2 Stir the prawns into the mixture and marinate for 10–30 minutes.

3 Separate the lettuce leaves and arrange on a serving plate. Spoon a couple of prawns and a little of the marinade onto each lettuce leaf.

½ **POINTS** value per serving
3½ **POINTS** values per recipe

24 calories per serving

Takes **10 minutes** + marinating

✻ not recommended

Smoked Fish Pâté

Serve this low *POINTS* value fish pâté with a zero *POINTS* value mixed salad, or with 1 medium (35 g/1¼ oz) slice of toast per person, for 1 extra *POINTS* value per serving.

Serves 4

400 g (14 oz) smoked haddock
1 bay leaf
4 tablespoons 0% fat Greek yogurt
1 tablespoon horseradish sauce
1 teaspoon wholegrain mustard
1 tablespoon chopped fresh parsley
1 tablespoon chopped fresh chives or spring onions
freshly ground black pepper
1–2 teaspoons lemon juice, according to taste

To garnish
lemon slices
parsley or chives

1½ *POINTS* values per serving
6½ *POINTS* values per recipe

105 calories per serving

Takes 20 minutes to prepare, 8 minutes to cook

✱ not recommended

1 Place the haddock in a shallow pan with the bay leaf and cover with water. Heat until just simmering and then cook gently for about 6–8 minutes until cooked. The flesh should be opaque and flake easily when tested with a fork.

2 Lift the fish from the pan and let it cool down. Flake it with a fork, removing the skin and any bones. Put it into a bowl and mash thoroughly with a fork.

3 Add the yogurt, horseradish sauce, mustard, parsley and chives or spring onions to the fish. Season with black pepper and stir together to mix thoroughly. Taste, adding a little lemon juice, if needed. The pâté should be salty enough, but add a little extra salt if you wish.

4 Pack the pâté into individual dishes or ramekins, or put it into one large dish. Cover and refrigerate until ready to serve. Garnish with lemon slices and parsley or chives.

Variation This pâté is delicious when smoked mackerel is used instead of haddock. This fish is already cooked. You can buy the fillets from the deli section at your supermarket. Just remove the skin and any bones as before. If you use smoked mackerel, the *POINTS* values will be 7 per serving because the fish is oily.

Mini Meatballs with Spicy Dipping Sauce

These make great party nibbles or you can serve them as a starter to share for an informal dinner.

Serves 4

For the meatballs
200 g (7 oz) lean steak mince
2 tablespoons snipped chives
2 tablespoons finely chopped fresh parsley
1 egg white
low fat cooking spray
salt and freshly ground black pepper

For the dipping sauce
227 g can chopped tomatoes with garlic
2 tablespoons tomato purée
1 teaspoon chilli powder

2 *POINTS* values per serving
7 *POINTS* values per recipe

89 **calories** per serving

Takes **20 minutes** to prepare,
25 minutes to cook

* meatballs only

1 In a bowl, mix together the mince, chives, parsley and egg white until well combined. Season. Using wet hands, shape into 12 equal sized balls.

2 Lightly coat a non stick frying pan with the cooking spray and heat until hot. Add the meatballs and cook, turning occasionally, for 8–10 minutes until browned and cooked through (you may need to do this in batches – keep all the meatballs warm as you do so).

3 Combine the sauce ingredients and heat in a small pan for 2–3 minutes until hot.

4 Serve the meatballs with cocktail sticks for dipping into the sauce.

Tips For a main course for two, serve the hot meatballs and sauce on top of 300 g (10½ oz) cooked pasta, for a *POINTS* value of 5½ per serving.

Each meatball will be ½ *POINTS* value.

Houmous with Pitta

This has all the flavour of shop-bought varieties but just a fraction of the **POINTS** values.

Serves 6

400 g can chick peas, drained and 2 tablespoons of liquid reserved
1 large garlic clove, chopped roughly
2 teaspoons toasted sesame oil or olive oil
2 tablespoons lemon juice
salt and freshly ground black pepper

To serve
chopped fresh coriander or parsley
6 mini pitta breads

---

2 POINTS values per serving
13 POINTS values per recipe

C   **130 calories** per serving

Takes **10 minutes**

V

✻   not recommended

1 Tip the chick peas into a blender or food processor with the reserved liquid. Alternatively, mash the chick peas and reserved liquid with a potato masher. Add the garlic, sesame or olive oil and lemon juice, and then blend for about 20 seconds until the mixture is smooth.

2 Transfer the mixture to a serving bowl, adding seasoning according to taste. You may wish to add a little more lemon juice too. Sprinkle with the chopped coriander or parsley.

3 Warm the pitta breads under the grill or in a toaster. Serve with the houmous.

Variation If you want to reduce the **POINTS** values to 1 per serving, serve the houmous with zero **POINTS** value vegetable crudités instead of the pitta bread.

Tomato, Thyme and Goat's Cheese Tartlets

These bite-sized tartlets are very moreish, and will soon disappear at a party. The recipe uses the individual kind of goat's cheese that has a soft edible white rind like Brie.

Makes 18

low fat cooking spray
2 x 45 g sheets frozen filo pastry, defrosted
100 g goat's cheese, diced
150 g (5½ oz) cherry tomatoes, halved
1 tablespoon freshly chopped thyme
1 egg, beaten
125 ml (4 fl oz) skimmed milk
salt and freshly ground black pepper

1 POINTS value per serving
15½ POINTS values per recipe

C **40 calories** per serving

Takes **15 minutes** to prepare,
15 minutes to cook

V

* not recommended

1 Preheat the oven to Gas Mark 4/180ºC/fan oven 160ºC. Lightly spray the hollows of two mini muffin tins with the cooking spray.

2 Layer up the filo sheets, misting with the cooking spray in between. Cut into 18 x 8 cm (3¼ inch) squares and press into the mini muffin tins. Bake for 3–4 minutes until crisp and golden.

3 Divide the goat's cheese, cherry tomatoes and thyme between the pastry cases, then mix the egg and milk together with seasoning and carefully pour into the tartlets.

4 Bake for 13–15 minutes on the centre shelf until the filling is set. Carefully remove from the tin and serve warm.

Variation You can also use the same quantity of crumbled Feta cheese, in place of the goat's cheese, for ½ **POINTS** value per serving.

Photo For Sausage Rolls recipe, see p102.

Sausage Rolls

Always a popular item at parties, these sausage rolls will disappear fast when served warm from the oven.

Makes 16

250 g (9 oz) plain flour
125 g (4½ oz) low fat spread
8 thick, low fat sausages
1 onion, grated
1 teaspoon wholegrain mustard
low fat cooking spray
1 tablespoon skimmed milk, to glaze
salt and freshly ground black pepper

2 *POINTS* values per serving
31½ *POINTS* values per recipe

116 **calories** per serving

Takes **15 minutes** to prepare + chilling,
20 minutes to cook

✱ recommended

1 Reserve 1 tablespoon of flour for rolling out the pastry, then sift the remainder into a bowl with a pinch of salt.

2 Rub in the low fat spread until the mixture resembles breadcrumbs, then add just enough cold water to bring the pastry together. Wrap in cling film and chill for 30 minutes. Preheat the oven to Gas Mark 4/180°C/fan oven 160°C.

3 Split the sausage skins and then squeeze the sausage meat out and mix with the onion, mustard and seasoning.

4 Dust the work surface with the reserved flour and roll out the pastry to a rectangle measuring around 24 x 37 cm (9½ x 14½ inches). Cut into two long strips and add the sausage meat filling down the length of each piece of pastry. Dampen the edges with water and roll the pastry around the filling, pressing to seal.

5 Lightly spray a non stick baking tray with the cooking spray. Slice each long roll into eight pieces and place on the tray. Brush with milk and bake for 20 minutes until golden brown and crisp.

Tortilla Chips and Dips

These Mexican style tortilla chips make very tasty nibbles when you have guests. The **POINTS** values are kept to a minimum because they're baked, rather than deep fried.

Serves 6
4 plain soft flour tortillas
low fat cooking spray

For the sour cream style dip
150 g (5 oz) half fat crème fraîche
1 tablespoon chopped fresh chives
freshly ground black pepper

For the chilli dip
1 small red onion, chopped very finely
¼ cucumber, chopped very finely
1 green chilli, de-seeded and chopped finely
juice of a lime or ½ a lemon
½ teaspoon sugar
salt and freshly ground black pepper

2½ **POINTS** values per serving
15½ **POINTS** values per recipe

C 212 calories per serving

Takes **10 minutes** to prepare,
10 minutes to cook

V

✳ not recommended

1. Preheat the oven to Gas Mark 6/200°C/fan oven 180°C.

2. Stack the tortillas into a pile and cut them into quarters. Cut each quarter into three or four pieces. Spread out the pieces on baking sheets and spray them with the cooking spray – do this in batches if you need to.

3. Bake for 8–10 minutes, until the tortilla chips are crisp and golden.

4. Meanwhile, make the dips. For the sour cream style dip, combine the crème fraîche and chives. Season with a little black pepper. For the chilli dip, mix together the onion, cucumber, chilli, lime or lemon juice, sugar and seasoning. Transfer the dips to separate serving bowls.

5. Cool the tortilla chips, and then serve with the dips.

Tip Flavour plain soft tortillas with a little chilli powder and mixed dried herbs. Lightly spray the tortillas with the cooking spray and then sprinkle on the zero **POINTS** value flavourings.

Quiche with a Difference

Who says a quiche has to have pastry? This recipe works well for picnics too.

Serves 8

low fat cooking spray
1 onion, sliced into thin rings
75 g (2¾ oz) mushrooms, sliced
5 eggs, beaten
100 ml (3½ fl oz) skimmed milk
250 g (9 oz) cottage cheese
2 tomatoes, sliced
40 g (1½ oz) mature Cheddar cheese, grated
1 tablespoon parsley, chopped
salt and freshly ground black pepper

2 POINTS values per serving
16½ POINTS values per recipe

121 calories per serving

Takes **10 minutes** to prepare,
40 minutes to cook

V

✳ recommended

1 Heat a non stick wok or large frying pan and spray with the cooking spray. Fry the onion and mushrooms for a couple of minutes until soft, adding a little water if necessary to stop them sticking.

2 Meanwhile, preheat the oven to Gas Mark 5/190°C/fan oven 170°C and spray a 25 cm (10 inch) metal flan dish with the cooking spray.

3 Put the onion and mushrooms in the flan dish. Mix together the eggs, milk and cottage cheese, season and pour this over the onion and mushroom mixture.

4 Arrange the sliced tomatoes on the top and sprinkle the Cheddar cheese and parsley over the tomatoes.

5 Bake for 30–40 minutes until set and golden brown. Allow to cool a little before cutting into eight slices and removing from the dish.

Tip For a picnic or lunchbox, either take the whole quiche in its dish or cut it into portions and wrap in foil. It will keep for a couple of days in the fridge.

Cheesy Garlic Mushrooms

Keep this easy starter in mind for a special supper – it's quick but impressive. These are also great to hand around at parties.

Serves 4

10 large cup shaped field mushrooms, preferably portabello
200 g (7 oz) low fat soft cheese with garlic and herbs or onion and chives
4 cherry tomatoes, chopped
2 tablespoons soy sauce
a small bunch of parsley, chopped finely
salt and freshly ground black pepper

1½ *POINTS* values per serving
5 *POINTS* values per recipe

93 calories per serving

Takes **10 minutes** to prepare, **20 minutes** to cook

V

✱ not recommended

1 Preheat the oven to Gas Mark 4/180°C/fan oven 160°C and remove the stalks from eight of the mushrooms. Chop the stalks and the two whole mushrooms finely and place in a bowl with the soft cheese, tomatoes, soy sauce and seasoning and most of the parsley (reserving a little for the garnish).

2 Beat the mixture together with a wooden spoon. Place the destalked mushrooms cup side up in a baking dish.

3 Pile the cheese mixture into each mushroom and bake for 20 minutes, then serve scattered with the rest of the parsley.

Tip Mushrooms have a distinct flavour. In order to retain the full flavour of the mushrooms you should not wash them, but rather gently wipe them clean with a damp cloth and then dry them with a paper towel.

Thai Fish Cakes with Sweet Chilli Dip

Eat these with your fingers, dipping the fish cakes into a bowl of sweet and hot sauce.

Serves 4

2 dried Kaffir lime leaves or zest of a small lemon
2 tablespoons boiling water
300 g (10½ oz) cod fillets
100 g (3½ oz) frozen cooked prawns, thawed
1 tablespoon red or green curry paste
a small bunch of fresh coriander
100 g (3½ oz) green beans, thawed if frozen, chopped into fine rings
1 teaspoon salt
low fat cooking spray

For the sweet chilli dip

1 small cucumber, quartered lengthways
1 small chilli, de-seeded and sliced finely
2 teaspoons caster sugar
3 tablespoons rice vinegar or white wine vinegar
fresh coriander leaves, to garnish

2 *POINTS* values per serving
7½ *POINTS* values per recipe

115 calories per serving

Takes 15 minutes to prepare
+ 10 minutes–1 hour chilling,
20 minutes to cook

✳ not recommended

1 Soak the lime leaves in the boiling water for 5 minutes, drain and then chop finely.

2 Put the fish, prawns, curry paste, lime leaves or lemon zest and coriander in a food processor and chop to a fine paste, then add the beans and salt and pulse to mix in. Transfer to a clean bowl, cover with cling film and refrigerate for up to an hour, though 10 minutes will do.

3 Meanwhile, to make the dip, finely slice the cucumber and put in a bowl with the chilli. Combine the sugar, vinegar and 1 tablespoon water in a saucepan and heat until the sugar has dissolved. Leave to cool, then pour over the cucumber. Spoon into little dipping bowls and garnish with the coriander leaves.

4 Lightly oil your hands to stop the fish cake mixture sticking to them, then take a tablespoon of the fish mixture at a time and shape into a small patty.

5 Heat a non stick frying pan and spray with the cooking spray, then fry the fish cakes, a few at a time, for 5 minutes on each side until golden and cooked through. Lift out with a fish slice and keep warm while you cook those remaining. Serve with the dipping sauce.

Baby Potato Bites

These little roasted potatoes topped with tasty toppings will go down a treat with everyone.

Makes 16

8 x 40 g (1½ oz) potatoes (e.g. Charlotte)
2 tablespoons olive oil
coarse ground salt and freshly ground black pepper

For the coronation chicken topping
25 g (1 oz) cooked skinless chicken, chopped
1 tablespoon chopped red pepper
2 tablespoons virtually fat free fromage frais
1 teaspoon curry paste
1 teaspoon mango chutney
chopped fresh parsley, to garnish

For the crème fraîche and chilli topping
2 tablespoons half fat crème fraîche
1 teaspoon finely chopped green chilli
1 spring onion, chopped finely

For the prawn and tomato salsa topping
2 tablespoons fresh tomato salsa
8 cooked prawns
4 tiny sprigs of fresh coriander

1 *POINTS* value per serving
16 *POINTS* values per recipe

C **35 calories** per serving

Takes **15 minutes** to prepare,
30–40 minutes to cook

V (crème fraîche and chilli topping only)

* not recommended

1 Preheat the oven to Gas Mark 5/190°C/fan oven 170°C. Toss the potatoes in the oil and tip into a shallow roasting pan. Season and roast for 30–40 minutes until tender. Leave until cool enough to handle.

2 Meanwhile make up the toppings – each is sufficient for four potato halves. Simply combine the ingredients together for each option, leaving some chopped herbs to garnish.

3 Cut the potatoes in half and then top with your choice of topping(s). Arrange on a plate and serve immediately.

Tip The potatoes can be cooked up to 2 hours ahead. Do not cut them in half until needed. Cool, cover and keep in the refrigerator. Either warm up before serving or serve them at room temperature.

Variation For the extra potato halves, try a blue cheese and chive topping for 1½ *POINTS* values per potato half. Mix together 25 g (1 oz) blue cheese, 1 tablespoon half fat crème fraîche and 1 teaspoon chopped chives.

Vegetable Samosas

Samosas are ideal for starters, snacks and buffets. Those served in Indian restaurants or bought from supermarkets are very high in **POINTS** values. These are baked to keep the **POINTS** values to a minimum.

Makes 20

275 g (9½ oz) potatoes, peeled and cut into 1 cm (½ inch) cubes
1 small carrot, peeled and chopped finely
low fat cooking spray
1 small onion, chopped finely
1 garlic clove, crushed
50 g (1¾ oz) frozen peas, defrosted
1 teaspoon medium curry powder
1 tablespoon chopped fresh coriander
5 x 15 g sheets of filo pastry (approximately 30 x 40 cm/12 x 16 inches), defrosted if frozen
salt and freshly ground black pepper

To serve

4 tomatoes, chopped finely
1 small red onion, chopped finely
2 teaspoons sesame oil
2 tablespoons chopped fresh mint

1 Bring a large pan of water to the boil and cook the potatoes and carrot for about 10 minutes. Drain well and then partially mash.

2 Spray a non stick frying pan with the cooking spray. Add the onion and garlic, and cook until lightly browned, adding a little water if necessary to stop them sticking. Mix the onion, garlic, peas, curry powder and coriander into the mashed potato and carrot mixture. Season and allow to cool. Preheat the oven to Gas Mark 4/180°C/fan oven 160°C. Spray two baking sheets with the cooking spray,

3 Lay the sheets of pastry on top of each other, misting with cooking spray in between, and cut into strips measuring approximately 30 x 10 cm (12 x 4 inches). Place a tablespoon of the samosa mixture at one end of a strip of pastry. Fold the corners over and over to make a triangle, enclosing all the filling. Repeat the process to make 20 samosas. Lay them on the baking sheets as you prepare them. Lightly spray the samosas with the cooking spray and then bake for 25–30 minutes, until golden. Meanwhile, mix together the tomatoes, onion, oil and mint and serve with the samosas.

½ **POINTS** value per serving
8½ **POINTS** values per recipe

C 35 **calories** per serving

Takes **30 minutes** to prepare, **30 minutes** to cook

V

✻ recommended

Tip Filo pastry soon dries out, so it's important to keep it covered as you work — use a clean, damp tea towel or cling film.

Variation Use mint in the samosas instead of coriander, if you prefer. The **POINTS** values will remain the same.

Chicken Satay Skewers

These are delicious eaten hot or cold, and are ideal for parties, packed lunches or picnics.

Serves 4

350 g (12 oz) skinless boneless chicken breast, chopped into bite size pieces
1 garlic clove, crushed
2 tablespoons dark soy sauce
1 teaspoon dried chilli flakes
2 tablespoons crunchy peanut butter
1 tablespoon tomato purée
100 ml (3½ fl oz) pineapple juice

1 Place the chicken in a shallow, non metallic dish.

2 Mix together the garlic, soy sauce, chilli flakes, peanut butter, tomato purée and pineapple juice. Pour the mixture over the chicken and toss well to coat all the pieces. Cover and leave to marinate for 30 minutes.

3 Preheat the grill to high. Thread the chicken pieces onto wooden skewers. Place them under the grill for 15 minutes, turning frequently, until evenly browned and cooked through.

3 *POINTS* values per serving
12½ *POINTS* values per recipe

160 calories per serving

Takes **10 minutes** to prepare, **15 minutes** to cook + **30 minutes** marinating

* recommended

Tip Soak the wooden skewers in water for 20 minutes before using, to prevent them from burning.

Simple Sushi

3 POINTS VALUE

Serves 4

200 g (7 oz) dried sushi rice, rinsed and drained
3 tablespoons rice vinegar
1 tablespoon granulated artificial sweetener
½ teaspoon salt
4 sheets seaweed
4 pea sized 'blobs' of wasabi paste, plus extra to serve
10 cm (4 inches) cucumber, peeled and cut into thin lengths
½ celery stick, cut into long strips
3 crab sticks, each cut in half lengthways
6–8 thin strips of red or yellow pepper
6 asparagus spears, tinned or lightly cooked

To serve
pickled ginger
soy sauce

3 POINTS values per serving
11 POINTS values per recipe

246 calories per serving

Takes **55 minutes**

* not recommended

1 Place the rice in a lidded, heavy based saucepan with 250 ml (9 fl oz) water. Bring to the boil and simmer for 10 minutes, stirring occasionally. Remove from the heat, cover and leave to stand for 15 minutes. Meanwhile, make your sushi vinegar by mixing together the rice vinegar, sweetener and salt.

2 Put the cooked rice into a large, non metallic bowl and use a plastic spatula to break up any lumps. Gradually pour in the sushi vinegar and continue to slice through the rice for 2–3 minutes to cool it a little. The rice should be sticky but not lumpy.

3 Place a sheet of seaweed, shiny side down, on a clean tea towel. Use damp hands to pick up a quarter of the rice and place it in the middle of the seaweed. Dampening your hands regularly, flatten the rice and spread it towards you so that it is about 2 cm (¾ inch) from the edge of the seaweed closest to you and up the sides. At the end it will be several centimetres from the back of the seaweed and about ½ cm (¼ inch) thick.

4 Put a blob of wasabi paste on your finger and wipe it from right to left along the rice, about 5 cm (2 inches) from the edge nearest you. Lay strips of cucumber along the wasabi. For the crabstick rolls, lay the celery and crab sticks alongside; for the vegetarian rolls, lay the red pepper and asparagus spears alongside. Trim any long ends later.

5 To roll the sushi, start with the edge nearest to you. Lift up the tea towel and ease the seaweed into a roll. You might have to tuck in the filling and uncovered seaweed. Continue to roll until all the seaweed has been wrapped around the filling. Move the roll to a board and trim the ends. Cut the roll into six and repeat for the rest of the seaweed. Arrange three of each roll on a plate and garnish with extra wasabi, pickled ginger and a dipping bowl of soy sauce.

Tip This recipe makes 24 rolls, for ½ **POINTS** value each.

Cheesy Chicken Goujons

These extra tasty chicken goujons are great for sharing.

4½ POINTS VALUE

Serves 4

4 x 125 g (4½ oz) skinless boneless chicken breast fillets
1 egg
2 medium slices bread (white or wholemeal)
50 g (1¾ oz) Parmesan cheese, finely grated
low fat cooking spray
salt and freshly ground black pepper

1 Preheat the oven to Gas Mark 7/220°C/fan oven 200°C. Slice each chicken breast into seven or eight finger-width strips. Beat the egg, with seasoning, in a shallow bowl.

2 Whizz the bread to crumbs in a food processor and mix with the grated Parmesan on a large plate. Dip the chicken strips first in the egg then in the cheesy crumbs to coat.

3 Place the chicken strips on a baking tray that has been lightly sprayed with the cooking spray, and mist the chicken goujons with a little more spray. Bake for 10–12 minutes until crisp, golden and cooked through.

4½ *POINTS* values per serving
17½ **POINTS** values per recipe

239 **calories** per serving

Takes **20 minutes**

recommended before cooking, if using fresh chicken

Chocolate Brownie Cake

Chocolate brownies are so delicious – and so moreish. Why not make a batch when you're inviting a few friends around, and then freeze any leftover for later.

Makes 16 slices

225 g (8 oz) cooking apples, peeled, cored and chopped
low fat cooking spray
100 g (3½ oz) self raising white flour
¼ teaspoon salt
60 g (2 oz) unsweetened cocoa powder
1 large egg
2 large egg whites
175 g (6 oz) light muscovado sugar
2 tablespoons vegetable oil
2 teaspoons vanilla extract

1 Cook the apples with 1 tablespoon of water in a small, lidded saucepan until very soft. Alternatively, cook them in the microwave on High for 3 minutes, stirring twice. Leave them to go completely cold and then mash with a fork or potato masher.

2 Preheat the oven to Gas Mark 4/180°C/fan oven 160°C. Spray a 23 cm (9 inch) square non stick baking tin with the cooking spray and line it with greaseproof paper.

3 Sift the flour, salt and cocoa powder in a bowl. In another large bowl, whisk together the egg and egg whites with the sugar. Stir in the apples, oil and vanilla extract.

4 Fold the flour mixture into the egg mixture using a large metal spoon, taking care not to over mix.

5 Transfer the cake mixture to the prepared baking tin and bake on the middle shelf of the oven for about 25 minutes, until just firm. To check that the cake is cooked, insert a fine skewer into the centre – it should come out clean.

6 Cool the cake in the tin for 15 minutes, and then cut it into 16 slices.

1½ **POINTS** values per serving
27 **POINTS** values per recipe

C 105 calories per serving

Takes **15 minutes** to prepare, **25 minutes** to cook

V

✱ recommended

Tip Take care when you fold the flour mixture into the wet ingredients, as over mixing can prevent the cake from rising.

Chocolate Mousse

You can't go wrong with chocolate mousse and these individual servings are just right for a gathering of family or friends.

Serves 6

100 g (3½ oz) good quality dark chocolate (70% cocoa solids), broken into pieces
3 egg whites

To decorate
175 g (6 oz) raspberries
mint leaves
1 teaspoon icing sugar

2 *POINTS* values per serving
12½ *POINTS* values per recipe

C **116 calories** per serving

Takes **15 minutes** + chilling

V

✱ not recommended

1 Put the chocolate in a large, heatproof bowl. Place the bowl over a saucepan of gently simmering water and heat the chocolate until melted. (Be careful not to allow any water into the bowl.) Remove the bowl from the heat and set to one side.

2 In a large, grease-free bowl, whisk the egg whites until stiff.

3 Using a large metal spoon, fold 1 tablespoon of the egg white through the warm chocolate to 'loosen' it, then fold in the remaining egg white. Fold very gently to avoid losing too much air.

4 Divide the mixture between six small serving glasses or dishes, allowing enough space to finish off with the raspberries. Refrigerate until set.

5 Serve, topped with the raspberries and decorated with mint leaves and a dusting of icing sugar.

Tip Egg whites will not whisk successfully if there is the slightest trace of grease, including egg yolk, in the bowl or on the beaters, so make sure everything has been washed in hot, soapy water before you begin.

Mocha Meringues

Coffee meringues look, and taste, decadent – sandwiched together with cream and chocolate.

Makes 8

2 egg whites
110 g (4 oz) caster sugar
2 teaspoons instant coffee, dissolved in
1 teaspoon hot water
40 g (1½ oz) dark chocolate
(minimum 70% cocoa solids)
75 ml (3 fl oz) whipping cream
2 teaspoons icing sugar, sifted

2½ POINTS values per serving
20 POINTS values per recipe

C **126 calories** per serving

Takes **20 minutes** to prepare,
1 hour to bake + **1 hour** cooling

V

✻ not recommended

1 Preheat the oven to Gas Mark 2/150ºC/fan oven 130ºC. Line two baking trays with non stick baking parchment.

2 In a clean, grease free bowl, whisk the egg whites until they hold stiff peaks. Add 1 tablespoon of the sugar and whisk until combined. Repeat with the remaining sugar and whisk until the meringue is stiff and glossy. Whisk in the dissolved coffee.

3 Spoon a tablespoon of the meringue onto the baking tray, flattening slightly. Repeat to make 16 rounds. Bake for 1 hour. Turn off the oven and leave to cool in the oven for a further hour.

4 To make the filling, melt the chocolate in a small saucepan over a medium heat. Whip the cream until it holds soft peaks. Stir in the chocolate and icing sugar. The cream will firm up as the chocolate sets, so when firm enough use the cream to sandwich the meringues. Serve two each.

Tip Store the unfilled meringues in an airtight container for up to 5 days.

Celebration Time

Menu Ideas

Valentine's supper Watercress, Prawn and Mango Salad (p124), Creamy Garlic Chicken (p135)
and Cream Hearts with Passion Fruit (p148).

Easter Sunday lunch Garlic and Rosemary Leg of Lamb (p138), Sesame and Orange
Roasted Carrots (p128), 'Roast' Potatoes (p125) and Chocolate Nests (p157).

Bonfire Night Creamy Vegetable Soup (p123), Three-bean Chilli with Wedges (p147)
and Toffee Apple Wedges (p152).

Veggie Christmas Spiced Cranberry and Orange Warmer (p122), Christmas Vegetarian Roast
with Cranberry and Apple Sauce (p130), Roasted Garlic Vegetables (p134)
and Christmas Mincemeat Filo Slices (p154).

Pick an event, choose some
recipes and celebrate

Spiced Cranberry and Orange Warmer

This fruity drink, suitable for all the family, will surely bring inner warmth to a chilly winter's night.

Serves 6

1 litre (1¾ pints) cranberry juice
300 ml (½ pint) freshly squeezed orange juice
2 cloves
1 cinnamon stick (approximately 5 cm/2 inches)
2 teaspoons demerara sugar
1 orange, halved and cut into slices

2 *POINTS* values per serving
11½ *POINTS* values per recipe

C **135 calories** per serving

Takes **10 minutes** + **5 minutes** standing

V

✱ not recommended

1 Place all the ingredients except the sliced orange in a saucepan. Heat gently for 5 minutes without letting the liquid boil. Switch off the heat and leave to stand for 5 minutes.

2 Carefully strain into a large heatproof jug, add the orange slices and serve in heatproof glasses or tumblers.

Tip If you have a slow cooker, transfer the heated juice, with the spices, to the preheated pot. It will keep warm for several hours without spoiling. Simply ladle out as required.

Creamy Vegetable Soup

Butternut squash gives this soup a wonderfully creamy, velvety texture. Serve swirled with a tablespoon of low fat natural yogurt and a few snipped chives for an extra ½ **POINTS** value per serving.

Serves 6

low fat cooking spray
3 leeks, trimmed, washed and sliced
3 large carrots, peeled and diced
1 butternut squash, peeled, de-seeded and diced
1 litre (1¾ pints) hot vegetable stock
300 ml (½ pint) skimmed milk
juice of ½ a lemon
salt and freshly ground black pepper

0 **POINTS** values per serving
1 **POINTS** value per recipe

C 124 calories per serving

Takes **15 minutes** to prepare,
20 minutes to cook

V

✱ recommended

1 Heat a large, lidded, non stick saucepan, spray with the cooking spray, add the leeks, cover and cook over a medium heat for 4 minutes until softened.

2 Add the remaining ingredients and bring to the boil. Cover, leaving the lid slightly ajar, and simmer for 20 minutes until the vegetables are tender.

3 Liquidise the soup in batches using a blender or hand held blender and return to the pan to warm through. Adjust the seasoning to taste and serve in warmed bowls.

Tip If you find butternut squash difficult to peel, invest in a 'U' shaped peeler – it makes life much easier.

Watercress, Prawn and Mango Salad

An unusual combination of ingredients that is sure to tantalise your taste buds.

Serves 2

1 large ripe mango, peeled

85 g bag of watercress or baby spinach or rocket or mixed leaves, shredded

100 g (3½ oz) cooked, peeled prawns

1 small red chilli, de-seeded and chopped finely or 2 pinches of dried chilli flakes

2 cherry tomatoes, sliced into thin wedges, to garnish

For the dressing
juice of ½ a lemon
1 teaspoon wholegrain mustard
2 tablespoons virtually fat free plain fromage frais
1 teaspoon tomato purée
salt and freshly ground black pepper

1 Slice the mango in half and remove the stone. Slice each half four or five times, leaving about 1 cm (½ inch) at the end so that the fruit can be fanned out.

2 Divide the watercress, spinach, rocket or mixed leaves between two serving plates or bowls.

3 Place one mango fan over the top of each pile of leaves and divide the prawns between the two plates or bowls.

4 Mix all the dressing ingredients together in a bowl and pour the mixture over the prawns, then sprinkle over the chopped chilli and garnish with the tomato wedges.

2½ **POINTS** values per serving
5 **POINTS** values per recipe

C **102 calories** per serving

Takes **20 minutes**

✳ not recommended

'Roast' Potatoes

You might find you actually prefer these to potatoes roasted in oil.

Serves 4

400 g (14 oz) potatoes, peeled and cut into medium chunks
low fat cooking spray
a pinch of paprika (optional)
salt and freshly ground black pepper

1 Preheat the oven to Gas Mark 5/190°C/fan oven 170°C.

2 Bring a pan of water to the boil and boil the potatoes for
6–8 minutes, until soft on the edges. Drain.

3 Spray a non stick baking tray with the cooking spray and put in the
preheated oven for 1 minute.

4 Place the well drained potatoes on the hot baking tray. Season and
sprinkle over the paprika, if using.

5 Spray with the cooking spray and bake for 40 minutes, until crisp
and beginning to brown at the edges.

1 POINTS value per serving
4½ POINTS values per recipe

C **80 calories** per serving

Takes **15 minutes** to prepare,
40 minutes to cook

V

✳ not recommended

Christmas Day Roast Turkey with Apples and Apricots

Our feast day of feast days when you can really push the boat out and eat this succulent, golden-roasted turkey with all the trimmings.

Serves 10

4 kg (9 lb) oven-ready turkey, without giblets
low fat cooking spray
1 large onion, chopped finely
4 garlic cloves, crushed
400 g can apricots in juice, drained and chopped roughly, reserving the juice
100 g (3½ oz) fresh breadcrumbs
a small bunch of sage, chopped
6 Cox apples, cored and cut into eighths
200 ml (7 fl oz) vegetable stock
salt and freshly ground black pepper

---

4 POINTS values per serving
39½ POINTS values per recipe

C **335 calories** per serving

Takes **30 minutes** to prepare,
2½ hours to cook + **10 minutes** resting

***** not recommended

1 Pull out any fat from inside the turkey. Season inside and out. Preheat the oven to Gas Mark 6/200ºC/fan oven 180ºC.

2 To make the stuffing, heat a non stick frying pan and spray with the cooking spray. Stir fry the onion for a few minutes, adding a little water if necessary to stop it sticking, until golden and softened.

3 Add the garlic and stir fry for a further minute, then add half the apricots, 4 tablespoons of their juice, breadcrumbs and sage. Season and stir together. Spoon this mixture into the neck end of the turkey and then truss (sew up the neck with string or strong cotton).

4 Place the turkey on a wire rack in a baking tray, cover with foil and roast for 2 hours.

5 Remove the foil and remove the turkey and the rack. Drain off all the fat from the tray. Add the apples, remaining apricots and juice and the stock to the tray. Replace the rack and turkey on top of the fruit and roast for a final 30 minutes uncovered.

6 To check the turkey is cooked, insert a skewer into the thickest part of the thigh. If the juices run out clear, not bloody, then the turkey is cooked. Place on a carving board, loosely cover with foil and allow the meat to rest for 10 minutes or so before carving.

7 Discard any fat from the juices left in the pan and serve with the roast turkey, cooked apples and apricots. Allow 3 slices (approx 150 g/5½ oz) of turkey per person.

Sesame and Orange Roasted Carrots

This easy side dish is delicious with roast meat; the orange perfectly accentuates the sweet carrot flavour and the sesame adds a little crunch.

Serves 4

350 g (12 oz) carrots, peeled and cut into thick chunks
low fat cooking spray
zest and juice of a large orange
1 tablespoon sesame seeds
salt and freshly ground black pepper

½ **POINTS** value per serving
1½ **POINTS** values per recipe

C 58 calories per serving

Takes **15 minutes** to prepare, **45 minutes** to cook

V

✱ not recommended

1 Preheat the oven to Gas Mark 5/190°C/fan oven 170°C.

2 Place the carrots in a single layer in a roasting tin. Lightly coat with the cooking spray, season and cook for 30 minutes.

3 Remove from the oven and sprinkle over the orange zest and juice. Return to the oven for a further 15 minutes until tender and beginning to brown.

4 Sprinkle over the sesame seeds and roast for another 5 minutes until the seeds are golden.

Tip Try adding 4 garlic cloves, halved, with the orange juice for extra flavour and no additional **POINTS** values.

Christmas Vegetarian Roast with Cranberry and Apple Sauce

Many families have at least one vegetarian in their midst so here's the Christmas dinner for them.

Serves 6

175 g (6 oz) dried brown basmati rice or basmati and wild rice mix
low fat cooking spray
2 garlic cloves, crushed
1 large onion, chopped finely
2 carrots, peeled and grated
150 g (5½ oz) mushrooms, chopped
3 tablespoons soy sauce
100 g (3½ oz) fresh breadcrumbs
50 g (1¾ oz) unsalted hazelnuts, chopped
2 eggs, beaten
a small bunch of rosemary or thyme, chopped finely
salt and freshly ground black pepper

For the cranberry and apple sauce
200 g (7 oz) frozen cranberries
300 ml (½ pint) apple juice
2 tablespoons artificial sweetener

4 *POINTS* values per serving
23 *POINTS* values per recipe

C 315 calories per serving

Takes **20 minutes** to prepare,
1 hour 45 minutes to cook

V

✱ recommended

1 Bring a pan of water to the boil and cook the rice for 30–35 minutes, until just tender. Rinse and drain well.

2 Meanwhile, heat a large, non stick saucepan and spray with the cooking spray. Stir fry the garlic and onion for 5 minutes, until golden and softened, adding a little water if necessary to stop them sticking.

3 Preheat the oven to Gas Mark 4/180°C/fan oven 160°C. Add the carrots, mushrooms and soy sauce to the onion mixture and remove from the heat. Stir in the breadcrumbs, nuts, eggs, herbs, cooked rice and seasoning.

4 Spray a 900 g (2 lb) non stick loaf tin with the cooking spray. Pack in the mixture and bake for 1–1¼ hours, until firm and golden.

5 To make the cranberry sauce, bring all of the ingredients to the boil in a small saucepan and then simmer for 20–30 minutes, until the cranberries are broken down and the sauce is thick.

6 Cut the roast into slices and serve with the cranberry and apple sauce on the side.

Chinese New Year Roast Pork

Serves 4

500 g (1 lb 2 oz) pork tenderloin
300 ml (½ pint) pork, chicken or vegetable stock

For the marinade

2.5 cm (1 inch) fresh root ginger, grated finely
2 garlic cloves, crushed
2 tablespoons soy sauce
2 tablespoons Chinese red vinegar or balsamic vinegar
½ teaspoon Chinese 5 spice powder
½ tablespoon Szechuan pepper or freshly cracked black pepper

For the vegetable fried rice

200 g (7 oz) dried brown rice
low fat cooking spray
2.5 cm (1 inch) fresh root ginger, chopped finely
2 garlic cloves, diced finely
a bunch of spring onions, sliced finely
100 g (3½ oz) frozen peas
100 g (3½ oz) frozen sweetcorn
150 ml (¼ pint) vegetable stock or water
2 carrots, peeled and diced finely
100 g (3½ oz) canned pineapple in juice, drained and chopped
1 tablespoon soy sauce

6 POINTS values per serving
23½ POINTS values per recipe

C **454 calories** per serving

Takes **20 minutes** to prepare + **30 minutes** marinating, **40 minutes** to cook

✱ not recommended

1 Put the pork in a roasting tin. Mix all the marinade ingredients together in a small bowl then pour over the pork. Cover with foil and leave to marinate for 30 minutes in the fridge.

2 Meanwhile, preheat the oven to Gas Mark 7/220°C/fan oven 200°C. Put the rice on to cook in plenty of water, bring to the boil and simmer for 35 minutes or until tender, then drain.

3 Uncover the pork and pour the stock around it. Roast for 40 minutes or until cooked through, spooning the juices over it twice or so during the cooking. Once cooked, remove from the oven. Leave to rest in the tin for 15 minutes before serving.

4 Make the vegetable rice by spraying a large, lidded, non stick frying pan or wok with the cooking spray then stir fry the ginger, garlic and spring onions for a few minutes. Stir in all the other ingredients including the rice.

5 Cover the pan and cook for 2–3 minutes, then serve with the pork, sliced thinly (4–5 slices per person), with the juices left in the roasting tin drizzled over.

St Patrick's Day Colcannon Cakes with Turkey Rashers

Traditional Irish potato dishes are plentiful and delicious. The feast day of St Patrick, patron saint of Ireland, falls on the 17th March.

Serves 4

500 g (1 lb 2 oz) floury potatoes such as Maris Piper or Red Rooster, peeled and cut into even size chunks
50 ml (2 fl oz) skimmed milk
low fat cooking spray
1 small green cabbage, shredded
8 turkey rashers
salt and freshly ground black pepper

To serve

200 g (7 oz) watercress
2 tablespoons reduced sugar redcurrant jelly

2½ *POINTS* values per serving
11 *POINTS* values per recipe

C **200 calories** per serving

Takes **10 minutes** to prepare,
30 minutes to cook

✳ not recommended

1 Put the potatoes in a large saucepan of water. Bring to the boil and then simmer for 15–20 minutes, until the potatoes are tender. Drain and mash with seasoning and the milk.

2 Meanwhile, heat a large, lidded, non stick saucepan, spray with the cooking spray and add the cabbage. Stir fry for a few minutes and then add enough water to cover the bottom of the pan. Cover and allow to steam for 8–10 minutes, until softened.

3 Drain the cabbage and add to the potatoes with more seasoning if necessary and mix together. Leave until cool enough to handle and then, using your hands, shape the colcannon into eight patties. Preheat the grill to medium hot. Place the cakes under the hot grill to brown for about 3 minutes on each side.

4 Meanwhile, grill the turkey rashers as directed on the packet. Serve each colcannon cake with a pile of watercress, turkey rashers and the redcurrant jelly.

Roasted Garlic Vegetables

These are great served with roast meat or use them as an accompaniment to a vegetarian main course.

Serves 6

low fat cooking spray

2 large aubergines, sliced in half lengthways and then diagonally into thick slices

450 g (1 lb) courgettes, sliced fairly thickly

2 red peppers, de-seeded and cut into 6 lengthways

2 yellow peppers, de-seeded and cut into 6 lengthways

2 garlic bulbs, cut in half crossways and wrapped individually in foil

200 g (7 oz) dried bulgur wheat

a small bunch of fresh basil, mint or parsley, chopped roughly

2 tablespoons balsamic vinegar

salt and freshly ground black pepper

1 Preheat the oven to Gas Mark 7/220°C/fan oven 200°C. Spray two baking trays with the cooking spray and spread the aubergines, courgettes and peppers on them. Season and spray again with the cooking spray. Add the garlic parcels and bake for about 25 minutes.

2 Meanwhile, cook the bulgur wheat as directed on the packet, then drain and set aside.

3 Place all the roasted vegetables, with the bulgur wheat, herbs and any cooking juices on the baking trays, into a bowl.

4 Meanwhile, make the sauce. Unwrap the garlic bulbs and squeeze the pulp out of the skins into a food processor. Add 100 ml (3½ fl oz) of water, the balsamic vinegar and seasoning and blend to a smooth sauce.

5 Pour the sauce over the vegetables and bulgur wheat. Toss gently together and then serve.

 1½ **POINTS** values per serving
10½ **POINTS** values per recipe

C 180 **calories** per serving

⊙ Takes **15 minutes** to prepare, **45 minutes** to cook

V

✻ not recommended

Creamy Garlic Chicken

A luxurious recipe that is very quick to prepare, making it ideal for a special occasion. Serve with fine green beans and 100 g (3½ oz) new potatoes, for 1 extra **POINTS** value per serving.

Serves 2

2 x 165 g (5¾ oz) skinless boneless chicken breasts

40 g (1½ oz) Boursin light cheese

2 slices Parma ham

low fat cooking spray

175 g (6 oz) small tomatoes on the vine

1 teaspoon fresh thyme leaves

2 tablespoons balsamic vinegar

salt and freshly ground black pepper

1 Preheat the oven to Gas Mark 6/200ºC/fan oven 180ºC. Cut a pocket in the side of each chicken breast and stuff with the Boursin cheese. Season, then wrap a slice of Parma ham around each one. Place in a roasting tin and spray with the cooking spray. Roast for 10 minutes.

2 Remove the tin from the oven, add the tomatoes and spray them with the cooking spray. Sprinkle the tomatoes with thyme and seasoning and drizzle with 1 tablespoon of balsamic vinegar. Roast for a further 8 minutes or until the chicken is cooked through.

3 Lift the chicken and tomatoes out onto warmed plates, leaving behind any cheese. Add the remaining balsamic vinegar and 1 tablespoon of water to the tin. Place on a medium heat and whisk for 30 seconds to form a sauce. Pour over the chicken and serve.

4 **POINTS** values per serving
8 **POINTS** values per recipe

C 295 **calories** per serving

Takes 5 **minutes** to prepare, 20 **minutes** to cook

✱ not recommended

Marinated Trout Fillets with Apricot Couscous

The simple marinade used in this recipe can also be rubbed on lamb before grilling or used as a dip for crudités or roast vegetables. A side salad of watercress or rocket with ripe tomatoes, a squeeze of lemon juice and seasoning makes a wonderful accompaniment, for no additional **POINTS** values.

Serves 2

150 g (5½ oz) very low fat natural yogurt
2 cm (¾ inch) fresh root ginger, grated finely
2 garlic cloves, crushed
1 small red chilli, de-seeded and chopped finely
2 x 200 g (7 oz) trout fillets
50 g (1¾ oz) dried couscous
100 ml (3½ fl oz) boiling water
25 g (1 oz) dried apricots, chopped finely
a small bunch of parsley, chopped finely
zest and juice of a lemon
200 g (7 oz) cherry tomatoes, halved
salt and freshly ground black pepper

7 **POINTS** values per serving
14 **POINTS** values per recipe

C 340 calories per serving

Takes **15 minutes** to prepare,
10 minutes to cook + marinating

* not recommended

1 Mix together the yogurt, ginger, garlic, chilli and seasoning and rub it over both sides of the trout fillets. Chill and leave to marinate for at least 30 minutes, but up to 2 hours.

2 Preheat the grill to medium hot. Cook the fish under the hot grill for 4–5 minutes on each side, until golden and cooked through.

3 Meanwhile, put the couscous in a bowl and pour over the boiling water. Cover with a plate or other lid so that it will steam for 5 minutes.

4 Break up the couscous with a fork and stir through the apricots, parsley, lemon zest, lemon juice and seasoning. Serve the trout on a bed of couscous with the tomatoes on the side.

Garlic and Rosemary Leg of Lamb

Roast lamb is a traditional Easter dish – try this version and impress family and friends.

Serves 4

½ lean leg of lamb, approximately
  1 kg (2 lb 4 oz)
8 small sprigs of fresh rosemary
4 garlic cloves, sliced
1 orange, sliced thinly
1 tablespoon clear honey
salt and freshly ground black pepper

8½ *POINTS* values per serving
34½ *POINTS* values per recipe

C   **466 calories** per serving

Takes **10 minutes** to prepare + marinating,
1½ hours to cook + standing

✱ recommended

1 Rinse the lamb and pat dry. Place it in a shallow non metallic dish. Make slits all over the top of the lamb and insert the rosemary and garlic. Arrange the orange slices over the top and season well. Cover and leave to marinate for at least 3 hours or preferably overnight.

2 Preheat the oven to Gas Mark 6/200°C/fan oven 180°C.

3 Remove the orange slices from the lamb, move it to a roasting tin and cook for 1 hour.

4 Reduce the heat to Gas Mark 4/180°C/fan oven 160°C. Brush the lamb with the honey and cook for a further 30 minutes. Allow to stand for 15 minutes before carving.

Tip Use 1 kg (2 lb 4 oz) lean leg steaks in place of the joint, for a *POINTS* value of 6½ per serving.

Thai Infused Barbecued Tuna

Fresh tuna steaks are ideal to cook on the barbecue as the firm texture holds together well.

Serves 6
1 lime, cut into wedges, to serve

For the tuna
zest of a lime
1 red chilli, de-seeded and diced
1 tablespoon fresh root ginger, grated
½ x 25 g packet fresh coriander, chopped
1 tablespoon Thai fish sauce
6 x 100 g fresh tuna steaks
low fat cooking spray
freshly ground black pepper

For the noodle salad
a kettle full of boiling water
250 g (9 oz) dried thin rice noodles
2 carrots, peeled and grated coarsely
250 g (9 oz) beansprouts, rinsed
juice of a lime
2 tablespoons Thai fish sauce

3½ **POINTS** values per serving
22½ **POINTS** values per recipe

C 294 calories per serving

Takes **20 minutes** to prepare,
5–6 minutes to cook

✳ not recommended

1 Preheat the barbecue, giving it time to reach a moderate heat. Mix the lime zest, chilli, ginger and coriander with the Thai fish sauce, seasoning with the black pepper. Rub the mixture into the tuna steaks and leave until ready to barbecue.

2 Pour boiling water over the rice noodles in a large bowl and leave to soften for 4 minutes. Drain and rinse in cold water, then mix together with the carrots, beansprouts, lime juice and fish sauce.

3 When the barbecue has reached the desired cooking heat, lightly spray both the barbecue grill rack and the tuna steaks with the cooking spray. Place the tuna steaks on the grill rack and barbecue for 2–3 minutes on either side.

4 Serve the tuna steaks with the rice noodle salad, with extra lime wedges to squeeze over.

Tip You can also cook the tuna steaks on a griddle pan or under a grill preheated to medium hot. Cook for 3–5 minutes on each side or until cooked to your liking.

Stuffed Acorn Squash

Celebrate autumn with these lovely little individual stuffed squashes.

Serves 4

4 x 300 g (10½ oz) acorn squashes
200 g (7 oz) dried mixed wild and basmati rice
a small bunch of fresh parsley, chopped finely
1 garlic clove, crushed
4 ripe tomatoes, de-seeded and chopped finely
25 g (1 oz) ready to eat dried apricots, chopped
20 stoned black olives in brine, drained and
  chopped
50 g (1¾ oz) toasted flaked almonds
zest and juice of a lemon
salt and freshly ground black pepper

4 POINTS values per serving
17 POINTS values per recipe

C **386 calories** per serving

Takes **20 minutes** to prepare,
50 minutes to cook

V

✱ not recommended

1 Preheat the oven to Gas Mark 5/190°C/fan oven 170°C. Wash the squashes and pierce in several places with the tip of a knife. Bake for 30 minutes, until tender. Remove from the oven and leave until cool enough to handle.

2 Meanwhile, bring a pan of water to the boil and cook the rice for 10–15 minutes, until tender, and then drain.

3 Slice a lid off the top of each squash and keep to one side. Scoop out the seeds and discard. Scoop out some pulp from the centres but leave a thick shell. If the bottom is not flat, cut a thin slice off to make a firm base.

4 Roughly chop the pulp and place in a bowl. Add all the other ingredients, including the cooked rice and stir together. Pile back into the squashes and replace the lids on top of the filling.

5 Place the squashes in a shallow ovenproof dish and bake for 20 minutes, until golden.

Tip When choosing acorn squash, look for one that is heavy with smooth dull skin and no soft spots. Look for orange on the skin as this tells you it's mature and ready to use – but too much orange means it is over ripe.

Beef and Wild Mushroom Stroganoff

Serve this comforting casserole with a sweet potato mash, for an extra 1 **POINTS** value per serving.

Serves 4

low fat cooking spray

2 x 400 g (14 oz) rump steaks, visible fat removed and cut into thin strips

4 shallots, sliced in half lengthways and then into fine semi-circles

4 garlic cloves, crushed

500 g (1 lb 2 oz) wild mushrooms or a combination of wild and field or button and chestnut mushrooms

a small bunch of thyme, stalks removed and leaves chopped

2 tablespoons tomato purée

2 tablespoons Dijon mustard

a small bunch of parsley, chopped roughly

200 g (7 oz) half fat crème fraîche

½ teaspoon paprika

salt and freshly ground black pepper

---

7 POINTS values per serving
27½ POINTS values per recipe

C **405 calories** per serving

Takes **20 minutes** to prepare,
5 minutes to cook

✱ recommended

1 Heat a large, non stick pan and spray with the cooking spray. Season the steak strips and fry a handful over a high heat until browned all over. Remove to a plate and repeat, frying the rest of the meat in batches.

2 Spray the pan again with the cooking spray. Fry the shallots and garlic until soft, adding a little water if necessary to stop them sticking.

3 Add the mushrooms, thyme, seasoning and the tomato purée and cook, stirring, for 1 minute.

4 Return all the steak to the pan with any juices, add the mustard and parsley and mix together.

5 Stir in the crème fraîche and cook on a low heat for 5 minutes, then stir in the paprika. Check the seasoning and serve.

Tip To make sweet potato mash for 4, peel and chop approximately 300 g (10½ oz) of sweet potatoes. Bring a pan of water to the boil and cook the potatoes for 15–20 minutes until tender. Drain and mash with seasoning.

Sausage and Lentil Casserole

How about preparing this recipe for Guy Fawkes night? It can be made well in advance, leaving you time to concentrate on other noisier bangers on the night. Serve with a generous spoonful of mashed swede, for no additional **POINTS** values.

Serves 4

450 g packet low fat pork sausages
1 large onion, chopped
1 garlic clove, crushed
1 large carrot, peeled and coarsely grated
175 g (6 oz) dried Puy lentils
fresh thyme, to taste
400 g can chopped tomatoes
600 ml (1 pint) hot beef stock
4 tablespoons half fat crème fraîche
salt and freshly ground black pepper

 **6 POINTS** values per serving
24½ POINTS values per recipe

C **325 calories** per serving

Takes **15 minutes** to prepare,
30 minutes to cook

* recommended

1 Prick the sausages all over, then dry fry in a non stick saucepan, until lightly coloured.

2 Add the onion to the pan and continue to stir fry until the onion is softened and golden. Add the garlic and carrot and cook for a further minute.

3 Stir in the lentils, thyme, tomatoes and stock. Bring to the boil, then reduce the heat to a gentle simmer and cook, uncovered, for 30 minutes. Stir occasionally, adding a drop of water if the mixture becomes too dry. Season to taste.

4 When the casserole is ready to serve, stir in the crème fraîche.

Tip Puy lentils can be found in most supermarkets. They require no soaking and taste great. Green lentils or continental lentils are a good substitute.

Variation V For a vegetarian option, use 8 Quorn sausages and replace the beef stock with vegetable stock. The **POINTS** values per serving will be 4.

Roast Beef with Yorkshire Puddings

Serve with the 'Roast' Potatoes on page 125.

Serves 6

2 tablespoons English mustard powder
1 beef joint e.g. sirloin, rib or topside, weighing
  approximately 1 kg (2 lb 4 oz), boned and rolled

For the Yorkshire puddings
1 egg
150 ml (¼ pint) skimmed milk
a pinch of salt
50 g (1¾ oz) plain flour
low fat cooking spray

For the gravy
1 tablespoon plain flour
300 ml (½ pint) stock

5½ *POINTS* values per serving
33 *POINTS* values per recipe

C 310 calories per serving

Takes **1 hour** to prepare,
1½ hours to cook

* not recommended

1 Preheat the oven to Gas Mark 7/220ºC/fan oven 200ºC. Rub the mustard powder all over the outside of the meat and place in a roasting tin, cut side down. For a medium-cooked joint, roast for 20 minutes then reduce the oven temperature to Gas Mark 4/ 180ºC/fan oven 160ºC and cook for another hour.

2 Meanwhile, make the Yorkshire pudding batter by whisking the egg with the milk and salt in a bowl then leave to stand for 15 minutes. Add the flour, whisk again until thoroughly mixed and leave to stand until ready to cook.

3 Remove the meat from the roasting tray and place on a carving board, cover with foil and leave to stand. Do not wash the tray.

4 Increase the oven temperature to Gas Mark 7/220ºC/fan oven 200ºC. Spray a 10–12 hole non stick Yorkshire pudding tin with the cooking spray and place in the oven to get hot. After 10 minutes remove, pour in the prepared batter and return to the oven for 15–20 minutes until risen and golden.

5 Meanwhile, make the gravy in the roasting tray. Place the tray on the hob over a high heat (use an oven glove as it will still be very hot). Sprinkle in the flour then pour in the stock. Scrape up all the juices stuck to the bottom of the tray with a wooden spoon and bring to the boil. Boil for 1 minute then strain into a serving jug.

6 Carve the beef and serve three medium slices (35 g/1¼ oz each) with the Yorkshire puddings and gravy.

Three-bean Chilli with Wedges

A colourful pot of chilli that is full of goodness.

Serves 6

low fat cooking spray
1 onion, chopped
3 mixed peppers, de-seeded and chopped roughly
6 x 250 g (9 oz) baking potatoes, each cut into 8 wedges
1 vegetable stock cube
3 garlic cloves, crushed
½ teaspoon hot chilli powder
1 teaspoon ground cumin
½ teaspoon smoked paprika (optional)
410 g can kidney beans, rinsed and drained
410 g can flageolet beans, rinsed and drained
410 g can haricot beans, rinsed and drained
2 x 400 g cans chopped tomatoes
salt and freshly ground black pepper
150 g carton 0% fat Greek yogurt, to serve

4½ **POINTS** values per serving
28 **POINTS** values per recipe

C 373 **calories** per serving

Takes **15 minutes** to prepare, **25 minutes** to cook

V

＊ recommended for chilli only

1 Preheat the oven to Gas Mark 7/220ºC/fan oven 200ºC. Heat a large, lidded, non stick frying pan, spray with the cooking spray, and cook the onion and peppers for 7 minutes until softened and browned.

2 Meanwhile, bring a large pan of water to the boil, add the potato wedges and vegetable stock cube and cook for 5 minutes, until just tender.

3 Drain the potatoes, then spread out on two baking trays and lightly mist with the cooking spray. Place in the oven and cook for 20–25 minutes until crisp, turning half way through.

4 Stir the garlic and spices into the onions and peppers, then add the beans, tomatoes and seasoning. Cover and simmer for 15–20 minutes.

5 Ladle the chilli into bowls, top each with a spoonful of yogurt and serve with the potato wedges to dunk in.

Cream Hearts with Passion Fruit

A beautiful dessert for a romantic night in with a loved one.

Serves 2

100 g (3½ oz) natural cottage cheese
50 g (1¾ oz) low fat soft cheese
50 g (1¾ oz) low fat natural yogurt
½ tablespoon artificial sweetener
¼ teaspoon vanilla extract
3 passion fruit
juice of ½ an orange

2 POINTS values per serving
3½ POINTS values per recipe

C **98 calories** per serving

Takes **15 minutes** + chilling

V

* not recommended

1 Line two 'coeur a la crème' moulds with small squares of muslin or clean thin cloth.

2 Smooth the cottage cheese by pushing it through a sieve with a metal spoon into a large bowl.

3 Add the soft cheese, yogurt, sweetener and vanilla extract. Beat with a hand held whisk for a minute or so.

4 Spoon the mixture into your moulds and leave overnight on a cooling rack over a plate in the fridge. Some of the liquid will drain out of the cheese mixture and the hearts will 'set'. Pour away any liquid.

5 To make the sauce, scoop out the seeds and pulp from the passion fruit and stir in the orange juice.

6 Just before serving, place a plate on top of one of the moulds and turn both over together. Gently lift off the mould, then the cloth from the cheese shape. Repeat with the second heart. Drizzle the sauce around the cream hearts and serve.

Tips 'Coeur a la crème' moulds are heart shaped and have small holes in their base to allow liquid to drain out. If you don't have moulds, you can line a colander or sieve with muslin. This way you will make one larger dome-shaped dessert rather than two heart-shaped ones – it will taste just as good.

The cream hearts are not easy to move once turned out, so position your plate carefully on the mould before turning it over.

Chocolate Torte

Absolutely delicious, this chocolate torte with its chocolate frosting will go down a treat with everyone.

Serves 8

12 Weight Watchers Double Chocolate Chip
  Cookies
40 g (1½ oz) low fat spread, melted
3 eggs, separated
75 g (2¾ oz) golden caster sugar
25 g (1 oz) cocoa
25 g (1 oz) plain flour
2 tablespoons chocolate spread
2 tablespoons low fat soft cheese

3½ *POINTS* values per serving
29 *POINTS* values per recipe

C 210 calories per serving

Takes **15 minutes** to prepare,
20 minutes to bake + **1 hour** cooling

V

✱ not recommended

1 Preheat the oven to Gas Mark 4/180°C/fan oven 160°C. Line a 19 cm (7½ inch) loose bottom, round tin with non stick baking parchment.

2 Whizz the chocolate cookies in a food processor to fine crumbs. Add the low fat spread and whizz again. Empty the crumbs into the prepared tin and, using your fingers or knuckles, press the crumbs evenly across the base to line. Set aside.

3 In a bowl, using an electric hand whisk, whisk the egg yolks and sugar until pale and fluffy. Then whisk in the cocoa and flour.

4 In another clean bowl, whisk the egg whites until they form soft peaks. Fold one third of the egg whites into the egg yolk mixture to loosen. Fold in the remaining egg whites until combined. Spoon into the prepared tin and level the surface. Bake in the oven for 20 minutes. Remove the torte from the oven and leave to cool for about 1 hour. (The cake will shrink down a little but don't worry.)

5 To make the chocolate frosting, gently warm the chocolate spread in a small saucepan and then mix in the soft cheese until smooth.

6 Remove the tin and the paper from the cake and transfer to a serving plate. Spread the chocolate frosting over the top, using a palette knife to swirl the frosting, if desired. Leave to set and then serve.

Toffee Apple Wedges

A special treat to pass around to friends.

Makes 24 wedges

225 g (8 oz) demerara sugar
1 tablespoon golden syrup
25 g (1 oz) butter
2 teaspoons lemon juice
2 tablespoons water
4 dessert apples, cored and quartered

1 Line two baking trays with non stick baking parchment. Have to hand some long handled tongs.

2 Place the sugar, syrup, butter, lemon juice and water in a heavy based saucepan and stir over a gentle heat until the sugar has dissolved.

3 Bring to the boil and boil rapidly without stirring for 5–10 minutes or until half a teaspoon of the mixture becomes hard and brittle when dropped into a bowl of cold water. (Take care to remove the pan from the heat before testing.)

4 Using the tongs, place half the apple wedges into the pan of toffee, making sure they are well coated. Remove, allowing the excess toffee to drip away. Spread the apples out onto the baking parchment. Repeat with the remaining wedges.

5 Leave to set in a cool dry place until serving. If wished, wrap each wedge in a piece of cellophane.

1 *POINTS* value per serving
22 POINTS values per recipe

C **55 calories** per serving

Takes **15 minutes** to prepare,
15 minutes to cook

V

✱ not recommended

Tip Take great care when making toffee as it gets extremely hot. Keep young children out of the way and supervise any older children who may wish to help.

Pancakes with Liqueur

Whisk up this easy all-in-one batter to make pancakes. It's the perfect recipe for Shrove Tuesday.

Serves 4

100 g (3½ oz) plain flour
a pinch of salt
1 egg
300 ml (½ pint) skimmed milk
finely grated zest and juice of a
 lime

finely grated zest and juice of a
 lemon
2 teaspoons vegetable oil
1 tablespoon caster sugar
2 tablespoons Cointreau,
 Grand Marnier or brandy

1 Sift the flour and salt into a large bowl. Add the egg, milk, lime and lemon zest and whisk together until smooth.

2 Heat a small, heavy based, non stick frying pan. Add a few drops of oil and pour in some batter, tilting the pan so that the mixture spreads over the base to make a thin pancake. When the pancake has set on the surface, flip it over to cook the other side. Make eight pancakes in this way, transferring them to a piece of kitchen towel as you cook them. When all the pancakes are cooked, fold them into triangles.

3 Wipe the frying pan with a piece of kitchen towel, then add the lime and lemon juice and sugar. Heat gently to dissolve, then add the liqueur or brandy. Return all the pancakes to the pan, overlapping to fit. Cook gently for about 1 minute. Serve two pancakes per person.

2½ *POINTS* values per serving
10½ *POINTS* values per recipe

C 195 calories per serving

Takes **10 minutes** to prepare,
15 minutes to cook

V

* not recommended

Christmas Mincemeat Filo Slices

Try these delicious, but easy, crisp flaky slices – a variation on mince pies which have all the usual delicious flavours but without the usual **POINTS** values. Serve with brandy butter, adding 1½ **POINTS** values per heaped teaspoon.

Makes 16

50 g (1¾ oz) walnuts, chopped
100 g (3½ oz) fresh brown breadcrumbs
50 g (1¾ oz) light muscovado sugar
400 g jar traditional mincemeat
2 dessert apples, peeled, cored and chopped
175 g (6 oz) cranberries
zest of an orange
50 g (1¾ oz) low fat spread, melted
270 g packet filo pastry, thawed
1 teaspoon icing sugar, for dusting

3 **POINTS** values per serving
45½ **POINTS** values per recipe

C 178 calories per serving

Takes **20 minutes** to prepare,
35 minutes to cook

V if using vegetarian mincemeat

* not recommended

1 Preheat the oven to Gas Mark 5/190ºC/fan oven 170ºC.

2 Mix together the walnuts, breadcrumbs and sugar. Preheat the grill to medium hot, line the grill pan with foil and spread the mixture out over the pan. Cook under the grill for 2–3 minutes, stirring from time to time until the crumbs are toasted. Leave to cool.

3 Mix together the mincemeat, apples, cranberries and orange zest. Stir in the crumb mixture.

4 Lightly brush a 23 x 33 cm (9 x 13 inch) Swiss roll tin with the melted low fat spread. Layer three sheets of filo in the base, then spread with half the mincemeat mixture. Arrange three more pastry layers on top, spread the remaining mincemeat on top and finally cover with the remaining pastry. Brush the top with the remaining low fat spread. Use a sharp knife to trim around the inside edge of the tin, discarding any overhanging pastry.

5 Bake for 35 minutes or until the pastry is crisp and golden. Cool in the tin before dusting with icing sugar and cutting into 16 slices.

Tips This is best served at room temperature.

Read labels carefully on food. Now that there are so many varieties of mincemeat available at Christmas, it is not surprising that very often the fat and calorie content go up with the price. Buy a traditional recipe that offers fewest **POINTS** values and check whether it contains animal suet if you wish to cook a vegetarian version.

Christmas Pudding with Brandy Sauce

Serves 10

low fat cooking spray
100 g (3½ oz) plain flour
1 teaspoon baking powder
100 g (3½ oz) low fat spread
300 g (10 oz) mixed dried fruit such as raisins, sultanas and currants (100 g/3½ oz of each)
100 g (3½ oz) dried apricots, chopped
100 g (3½ oz) caster sugar
100 g (3½ oz) fresh breadcrumbs
1 teaspoon ground cinnamon
1 teaspoon ground ginger
½ teaspoon ground cloves
½ teaspoon ground nutmeg
1 egg
150 ml (¼ pint) skimmed milk
2 tablespoons brandy

For the brandy sauce
40 g (1½ oz) cornflour
50 g (1¾ oz) dark brown sugar
600 ml (1 pint) skimmed milk
2 tablespoons brandy

1 Spray a 1.2 litre (2-pint) pudding basin with the cooking spray and line the base with a disc of non stick baking parchment. Sift the flour and baking powder into a bowl, add the low fat spread and rub in with your fingertips.

2 Stir in all the dried fruit, sugar, breadcrumbs and spices then mix in the egg, milk and brandy. Spoon into the prepared pudding basin and level the surface with the back of a spoon.

3 Cover with a double thickness of greaseproof paper with a pleat in the middle to allow for rising, and tie with string under the rim to secure. Place in a steamer or large saucepan a quarter full of boiling water and with a close fitting lid. Steam for 4½ hours. Turn out onto a serving plate.

4 Make the sauce in a saucepan, blending the cornflour with the sugar and a little of the milk. Add the rest of the milk, bring to the boil stirring constantly and cook for 2 minutes, still stirring, until thickened, then add the brandy, pour into a jug and serve.

4½ **POINTS** values per serving
46 **POINTS** values per recipe

C 310 calories per serving

Takes **30 minutes** to prepare,
4½ **hours** to cook

V

✱ not recommended

Tips You may feel there's enough brandy already in the pudding and sauce and prefer not to flame the pudding. However, if you want to flame the pudding to serve, after making the sauce place 2 tablespoons of brandy into a ladle and heat gently over a flame or electric ring. When it is warmed, pour over the pudding and ignite with a match.

Decorate it with a dusting of icing sugar and a sprig of holly. If you want to flame the pudding, remove the holly first.

Chocolate Nests

The perfect recipe for Easter.

Makes 8
125 g (4½ oz) dark chocolate
40 g (1½ oz) low fat spread
3 Shredded Wheat biscuits
24 mini chocolate eggs

1 Melt the chocolate and low fat spread together by putting them into a large heatproof bowl placed over a saucepan of gently simmering water. When smooth and melted, remove from the heat.

2 Break up the Shredded Wheat biscuits and stir into the chocolate mixture.

3 Spoon the mixture into paper bun cases, making slight depressions in the centre of each one to form a nest. Chill in the refrigerator until firm, about 20 minutes.

4 Serve with three tiny chocolate eggs in each nest.

3½ **POINTS** values per serving
25 **POINTS** values per recipe

C 170 **calories** per serving

Takes **15 minutes** + **20 minutes** chilling

V

* recommended

Tip You can reduce the **POINTS** values to 3 by having just 1 mini chocolate egg.

Index